MODERN DUNDEE

MODERN DUNDEE

Life in the City Since World War Two

ANDREW MURRAY SCOTT

breedon **books**
PUBLISHING

First published in Great Britain in 2002 by
The Breedon Books Publishing Company Limited
Breedon House, 3 The Parker Centre,
Derby, DE21 4SZ.

ISBN 1 85983 331 4

Printed and bound by Butler & Tanner, Frome, Somerset,
England.
Cover printing by Lawrence-Allen Colour Printers,
Weston-super-Mare, Somerset.

Contents

Acknowledgements

I would like to record my thanks to Deirdre Sweeney without whom this book would not have been written by me – and to my wife Frances who was unfailingly patient during the writing of it, offered helpful advice and tracked down many obscure reference queries.

I have been greatly assisted by the staff of the Local Studies Section, Dundee Central Library; the Librarian Eileen Moran, and Maureen Reid, Ida Glendinning, Carol Lamb and of course, Deirdre Sweeney.

I owe a considerable debt of gratitude to staff of D.C. Thomson & Co. Ltd, particularly the cheerfully patient Joyce Lorimer of the Photofiles Section at Kingsway East, also Calum Laird and Bill Moodie of the Syndication Department at Albert Square and Colin Stewart of the Offset Process Department.

I am extremely grateful for the courtesy of Alan Richardson in letting me use his excellent photographs and as ever for his professional advice and support.

I would also like to thank Iain Flett of Dundee City Archives, Sarah Craig, Press Officer of Tayside Police and Detective Superintendent Norrie Robertson of Tayside Police Crime Management, Petra Kydd of the City of Discovery Campaign, Bill Dower, Dundee College press officer, and Owen Daily, graphic designer at Dundee College, Susan McMartin of the National Lottery press office, Bill Whytock of Dundee City Chambers and Charlie Alexander, George Cabrelli, Harry Morrison, Lyn McDonald, Martin Horan, Norman Elder, Joe Fitzpatrick, Richard McCready and many others for advice, anecdotes, pictures or information which they kindly volunteered.

My deepest debt however is to the fourth estate; the generations of journalists of the Scottish press, particularly of the local publications of D.C. Thomson & Co. Ltd, whose painstaking daily efforts over the decades have created an invaluable archive of the city and her people to the benefit of posterity and this author.

Introduction

There can be few greater privileges than to be asked to compile a history of your home town and because I have mostly lived in Dundee the task became an intensely personal one. The lack of a narrative history of the city in the post-war period had often been noted and I felt a great responsibility bearing down on me, but what follows is of necessity a brief and subjective selection of, hopefully, the most important, dramatic or quirky events. I was often distracted and absorbed by material I had no possibility of finally including because of the word limit I was constrained by. Luckily, the publishers required a large number of photographs and this has allowed me to pack the book with evocative images; as they say, every picture is worth a thousand words.

It is broadly a social history; the story of Dundonians and those who have settled in Dundee, but the tale is interspersed with national and international events and how they have impacted on the city. The book would be very dull if I had concentrated exclusively on either the economic and industrial or the political, or if I had taken a purely nostalgic meander through the decades. I wanted to cover all these angles and more so that *Modern Dundee* would function as a 'good read' for the general reader, as a handsome gift for Dundonians abroad and as a well-researched reference work with enough hard facts and statistics to satisfy the history specialist. I hope that it is the kind of book which will be consulted both to decide pub arguments and as a starting point for research on specific topics of local history.

I dedicate the book to those who may recognise themselves on the pages that follow, whether in the foreground, just off the edge of the picture or somewhere between the lines – and to all those who have in any way enlivened the story of Dundee since World War Two.

AMS

Chronology of Important Dates

8 May 1945	VE day celebrations.
26 July 1945	General election results: socialist MPs Tom Cook and Lytton Strachey elected.
15 August 1945	VJ day celebrations.
26 May 1946	Princess Elizabeth opens Camperdown Park.
1947	Astral factory opens.
20 November 1947	Celebrations for royal wedding.
27 December 1948	The 'Fifie' *Sir William High* stuck on sandbank.
March 1949	Celebration sales to mark end of clothes rationing.
June 1949	Royal Highland Show, Riverside Park.
May 1951	Introduction of universal old-age pensions.
16 May 1951	*Campania*, Festival of Britain ship, in berth until 26 May.
6 June 1951	Biggest Tay-built tanker, *Aida* (13,500 tons), launched for trials.
28 August 1951	Bristol Brabazon flies over the city on test flight.
19 April 1952	Dundee FC lose (4-0) in Scottish Cup final to Motherwell but win League trophy back-to-back in 1951–2 and 1952–3 seasons.
September 1952	Dundee's Own exhibition at Caird Hall.
2 June 1953	10,000 flock to watch Coronation on TVs in Caird Hall.
January 1953	AEU organises strike of jute factory maintenance men and mechanics.
February 1953	Floods create demand for sandbags. 20 million ordered from Dundee; 24-hour working.
December 1953	J. Murdoch Wallace opens the JM Ballroom.
1954	First private houses built in Dundee by Bett Bros.
March 1954	Billy Graham crusade – relay services in Dundee.
1 May 1954	New obstetric and gynaecology research unit at Dudhope Terrace.
May 1954	Dundee Tattoo, Riverside Park.
July 1954	The *Fraser Fenton*, last of Dundee's trawlers, is sold.
13 February 1955	First public concert by City of Dundee Orchestra in Gaumont.
1 December 1956	Dick McTaggart wins gold at Melbourne Olympics.
25 December 1956	A public holiday for jute workers, in addition to two days at New Year.
6 August 1958	Arrival of diesel trains, Dundee drivers to be trained.
4 July–15 August 1959	Brighter Broughty Summer Festival: 20,000 on the beaches.
12 October 1959	National Mod in Dundee (previously 1913, 1937).
19 November 1959	Council approves clean air plan, Dundee to develop smokeless zones.
8 December 1959	*Mona* lifeboat disaster, eight men lost.
10 December 1959	W.E. Dryden opens first self-service food store in Dundee, Victoria Road.
15 January 1960	Dryburgh multis opened.
30 April 1960	Dundee United clinch promotion to First Division, defeating Berwick Rangers.
9 June 1960	Dundee Readymix Concrete Co. opened by Lord Provost McManus.
September 1960	Dundee's Own exhibition, Caird Hall.
January 1961	Demolition starts at the Overgate.
4 January 1961	Jute fire at King George Wharf, £250,000 damage.
12 May 1961	Astral open Gourdie factory.
4 August 1961	Foggeyley multis opened.
January 1962	DP&L suspend their Tay-Thames service.
June 1962	Polio outbreak in Fintry.
March 1963	Earl Grey Dock clearance for road bridge landfall. Royal Arch to be demolished.

1 May 1963	Dundee FC win first leg of European Cup semi-final, defeating AC Milan 1-0 at Dens.
7 October 1963	Beatles play Caird Hall, their first ever concert in a major hall.
25 April 1964	Dundee FC lose Scottish Cup final 3-1 to Rangers.
January 1965	Inner ring road, phase one, begins.
8 July 1965	Housing Convenor Tom Moore tops out the first Dallfield multi.
13 October 1965	Grampian TV begins broadcasting.
18 August 1966	Tay road bridge opened by the Queen.
April 1967	Bison factory opens at Trottick, to produce prefab building units.
July 1967	BBC 2 broadcasts in colour.
1 August 1967	Queens' College Dundee becomes Dundee University.
1 November 1967	Robert Francis Mone murders St John's teacher Mrs Nanette Hanson.
10 February 1968	Ferries *Scotscraig* and *Abercraig* towed to Southhampton.
30 May 1969	Royal visit by Queen and Duke of Edinburgh.
October 1970	Whitfield parish church foundation stone laid.
February 1971	Final phase of the 'new' Overgate centre opens.
15 February 1971	Decimalisation Day.
21 May 1971	Murder of eight-year-old Sharon Smith.
February 1972	Levi-Strauss open factory in Kilspindie Road.
August 1972	Murder of Leonard Pollington.
April 1973	Squatters move in to Peddie Street.
January 1974	Ninewells Hospital admits its first patients.
28 February 1974	General election victory of Gordon Wilson in Dundee East.
May 1975	The Barracuda opens on site of former JM Ballroom.
6 June 1975	First ever referendum in UK held on continuing as EEC member.
June 1975	NCR – 1,200 redundancies.
13 October 1975	Lord Provost Farquhar on trial for assault.
September 1976	NCR – 600 redundancies.
April 1977	Wallace's Auld Dundee Pie shop closes.
20 May 1977	Queen jostled by crowds at Camperdown Park during Silver Jubilee tour.
4 April 1978	Wellgate Centre opens.
March 1979	Referendum on Scotland Act.
3 March 1979	Jute fire at William Halleys, £1 million damage.
27 March 1979	Body of Carol Lannen found at Templeton Woods.
5 June 1979	Robert Christopher Mone convicted of murders of three women.
February 1980	High Court trial of former Lord Provost Moore, J.L. Stewart and J. Maxwell.
February 1980	Body of Elizabeth McCabe found at Templeton Woods.
May 1980	Council elections, Labour form administration with 25 of 44 seats.
May 1980	Redundancy packages offered to Robb Caledon workers.
19 May 1980	Roseangle Murders.
September 1980	Air Ecosse new service to Manchester.
March 1981	Council delegation to Nablus.
February 1982	Campaign against twinning with Nablus.
19 June 1981	Closure of the Odeon, formerly the King's Theatre.
8 April 1982	Rep's first production at Tay Square premises.
12 July 1982	Dundee paras welcomed home from Falklands.
November 1982	Dundee Project formed.
December 1982	Labour Party offices fire, Rattray Street.
8 September 1983	Prince Charles and Princess Diana in Dundee.
November 1983	Timex production record output on Sinclair Spectrum.
January 1984	Dundee becomes Enterprise Zone.
24 April 1984	Dundee Marathon.
October 1984	Sandy Kydd's anti-gravity machine hits the headlines.
January 1986	Closure of Dundee Ferries' 'ro-ro' terminal.
July 1986	Liz McColgan wins gold medal in 10,000 metres at Commonwealth Games.
20 May 1987	Dundee United play IFK Gothenburg in UEFA Cup final second leg at Tannadice.

8 March 1988	William Crowe convicted of murder of his wife at Arbroath Cliffs.
25 March 1988	Ford reject union compromise deal and abandon plans for Dundee factory.
7 July 1988	Piper Alpha disaster.
22 December 1988	PanAm flight 103 explodes over Lockerbie – Dundee drivers' accounts.
6 September 1989	Mrs Thatcher visits Dundee.
December 1990	Disappearance of Nealle Wilson.
January 1991	Dundee Textiles' finishing plant at Riverside opens.
April 1991	Start of James Martin/Labour clubs trial, Dundee Sheriff Court.
July 1991	Queen in Dundee to open EXPO 800.
4 July 1991	Royal Observer Corps stood down.
22 October 1991	Aberdeen–London express destroys Broughty level crossing gates.
31 December 1991	Octocentenary Hogmanay party, City Square.
January 1993	Discovery of headless corpse on Law.
30 January 1993	Timex dispute begins.
February 1993	Conviction of two regional councillors for fraud.
23 February 1993	Armed raid on GPO.
12 May 1994	John Smith addresses Labour conference in Caird Hall.
June 1994	European elections.
22 June 1995	Death of Lord Provost Tom McDonald.
27 June 1995	Royal Yacht *Britannia* at Dundee.
March 1996	Dunblane Massacre – Dundee condolence book.
December 1996	Dundee Book Prize launched.
31 August 1997	Death of Princess Diana.
September 1997	Devolution Referendum.
14 November 1997	New Muslim mosque opens in Miln Street.
7 April 1998	Death of James McIntosh Patrick.
20 October 1998	Professor Philip Cohen knighted at Buckingham Palace.
November 1999	Dundee Contemporary Arts building opens.
January 2000	Demolition work on DRI.
21 March 2001	Morgan Academy gutted by fire.
May 2001	The 'Provost Wright Affair' – resignation of Provost.
2 August 2001	Murder of Department of Employment officer Anne Nicoll on the Law.
11 September 2001	Broughty man Derek Sword among the dead in the World Trade Centre.
September 2001	Dundee Stars enter British Ice Hockey League.
24 October 2001	Professor David Lane knighted at Buckingham Palace.
March 2002	Announcement of £15m grant to build CIR building at Dundee University.

CHAPTER 1

The War and its Aftermath

Dundee's War

If every book is a journey then this roller-coaster ride starts quietly at the outbreak of war in 1939. Dundee was a small, tightly-knit community, yet the population of 165,000 was mostly filled with trepidation about the future. The city was defenceless and remarkably ill-provided with air-raid shelters. The Law Tunnel was examined for use as a public shelter. Retired architects offered other grandiose schemes and by the end of 1941 nearly 10,000 shelters had

September 1939: the evacuees assemble in King's Road. Over 11,000 mothers and children were evacuated. (The Courier, Dundee)

*The evacuees march to
the station. Note the
labels on luggage and
children.* (Evening
Telegraph, Dundee)

The evacuees march to the station. Note the labels on luggage and children. (Evening Telegraph, Dundee)

been constructed. The Corporation ordered attempts to camouflage landmarks
which might prove useful to Luftwaffe navigators. The Victoria and Stobswell
ponds were filled in. The Law Monument was framed with wood covered with
canvas which vandals promptly set on fire, creating a huge beacon visible for
miles! But nothing could be done about the Tay and the rail bridge, the most
prominent landmarks in eastern Scotland.

By July 1941, more than 19,000 local men had joined up to fight,
registering at the Employment Exchange in Gellatly Street. By the end of the
war, men were being drafted directly after their 18th birthday and up to the
age of 51. Some were exempted because they were in reserved occupations.
For these, there were always vacancies in the Police War Reserve, Auxiliary Fire
Service and first-aid teams. Conscription created a manpower shortage on the

home front but did not initially affect the unemployment levels, which suggests some local disaffection with the war effort.

There were conscientious objectors and these were interrogated by the South of Scotland Local Tribunal in Edinburgh. Mostly Jehovah's Witnesses like 24-year-old Hendry Carmichael or members of the Peace Pledge Union, or, like Thomas Faulkner and C.A. Coulston, lecturers at Queen's College, their ranks also included socialists like Robert Smith of Dura Street and Robert Ireland of North Wellington Street. They were ordered into non-combatant duties – agricultural work or the coal mines – although a small number were jailed.

Robert Grant, a 42-year-old Inland Revenue officer of Blackness Avenue, appeared at Dundee Sheriff Court in September 1940 on a charge of obtaining information useful to an enemy. Born in South Africa, Grant had visited Germany before the war and had German maps and drawings of aircraft in his home. He denied that he was a spy but witnesses claimed he had questioned sailors in a pub in Gellatly Street about navy manoeuvres. He was jailed for three months pending the question of internment. Another instance of disaffection concerned a deserter from the Pioneer Corps, 34-year-old John Fitzgerald of Atholl Street, who had not returned after home leave. A military escort had been sent to arrest him but the two spent a riotous day drinking and when they finally reached the railway station, Fitzgerald shot his escort and was later convicted of culpable homicide.

Schoolchildren building air-raid shelters in the Linlathen housing estate as part of the 'pick and shovel brigade'. The brigade mustered at Courthouse Square and was deployed to construct domestic and public shelters and later Anderson shelters when these were delivered to Dundee in prefabricated batches of 500. (Evening Telegraph, Dundee)

Women were conscripted into all of the services and most civilian jobs, including labouring, engineering and munitions. This eventually applied to women up the age of 50. There were 12 women working as welders at the Caledon yard. (Evening Telegraph, Dundee)

Dundee became a significant naval base, an important centre for munitions production and marine engineering. An entire fleet of 'Empire' cargo vessels was built in the Caledon yard for the Ministry of War Transport. Navy ships like HMS *Activity,* an 11,900-ton aircraft carrier, launched on 30 May 1943, rolled off the stocks as the shipyard worked around the clock, relatively unhindered by the severe air bombardment suffered by other centres of production. Dundee harbour was the home port of submarines and minesweepers. The Royal Navy's biggest submarines, *Thames, Clyde* and *Severn*, arrived in 1940 and ships of five nations, French, Dutch, Norwegian and later Russian, followed. The base was visited by Allied leaders including King Haakon and Crown Prince Olaf of Norway; General De Gaulle, leader of the Free French; General Wladyslaw Sikorski with three Polish generals and the Czech patriot Jan Mazaryk. King George, Queen Elizabeth and the Duke of Kent visited the base during the early years of the war. Molotov, the Russian Foreign Secretary, arrived secretly under cover of darkness for a meeting held in a railway carriage at the platform at the East Station.

These Allied sailors were billeted in the orphanage near Carolina Port, part of HMS *Ambrose,* a so-called 'stone battleship' which extended to Messrs Lindsay & Low's 'jam factory' at Carolina Port and other buildings. Across the river, at Woodhaven, remants of the base of the 70 to 80 Norwegian airmen who flew six Catalinas and Sunderland flying boats can still be seen along with the concrete anti-invasion blocks and the pillbox gun emplacements which stretch along the coast.

But the war came closest to most Dundonians through air raids. On 2 August 1940, 23 50kg anti-personnel bombs landed around Linlathen House.

The Polish submarine the Orzel (Eagle), which had made a daring escape from the Nazis across the North Sea, became the first craft to use the new Dundee submarine base. (Evening Telegraph, Dundee)

General de Gaulle decorates the crews of the Free French submarines Rubis and Minerve with the Croix de Guerre at Mayfield House. Later, de Gaulle inspected the Minerve and had difficulty traversing its narrow passages and tiny hatches. The dog is Bacchus, the mascot of the Rubis. (Evening Telegraph, Dundee)

The only fatalities were a cat and a flock of swallows. The *Courier* printed a derisory paragraph headed: 'Nazis say Dundee Was Bombed,' breaking the protocol of reporting raids on 'a North-East Scottish coastal town' or 'North-East Residential Town' whether Dundee, Monifieth, Montrose, Arbroath or Brechin.

On 24 September 1940, two 250kg bombs were dropped on the city. The first landed at the junction of Dalkieth Road and Nesbitt Street and the second in a vegetable patch at Montgomerie Crescent. Two men 30 yards from the first blast, Special Constable James Watson and an ARP warden, were saved by their 'tin lizzies' or steel helmets, although they suffered minor injuries. Two local residents, Mrs Inglis and Mrs Kidney, heard the whistle of the bomb and their house roofs sustained damage.

One month later, on 26 October, incendiary bombs were dropped over Dundee and there were three separate air-raid warnings during the night. 'In night raids on Scottish ports and industrial plants particularly violent fires were observed in Dundee…' ran part of an intercepted German High Command communiqué on 6 November 1940. It was a particularly optimistic piece of Nazi propaganda.

On 3 November, more than 30 aircraft flew over the city. The sirens sounded at 8pm, according to Robert Williamson, head air-raid warden of the

Repair work begins after the first 250kg bomb hit the junction of Dalkieth Road and Nesbitt Street. (Evening Telegraph, Dundee)

east end. Williamson was on duty during the next two nights of bombing which constituted the city's main air raids. At 9.04pm on 4 November, two bombs dropped harmlessly beside Drumgeith Cottage on the northern outskirts of the city, then a large, 1,000kg bomb landed behind the Taybank works in Arbroath Road. It destroyed an outhouse. The massive bomb – resembling in its bloated size the Luftwaffe commander, Herman Goering, and therefore known as a Herman – did not explode. It had been deflected off the sides of a turf shelter in which 60 female jute workers were sheltering. The fourth bomb – another Herman – landed in the north-east corner of Baxter Park near Dalkieth Road and burst a water main, creating a 15ft wide hole in the road and shattering most of the windows in the surrounding streets.

The following evening at about 8pm the sirens went off. Witnesses claim the first explosions preceded the sirens. Eight bombs were dropped in two clusters of four over the west end. The first landed at the west side of Faringdon Terrace and the second at the rear of the Fernbrae nursing home, causing substantial damage but no injury. The third bomb hit number 13 Briarwood Terrace, where the body of Mrs Elizabeth Cooper, a widow who was housekeeper to the Revd Andrew Moodie, was found after a two-hour search.

The scene at 13 Briarwood Terrace where Mrs Elizabeth Cooper was killed. The Revd Andrew Moodie and his daughter emerged virtually unscathed from the cellar. (The Courier, Dundee)

The fourth bomb landed without causing injury at the front of number 12 Marchfield Road. The first of the second string of bombs landed at the rear of 258 Blackness Road. The second, a direct hit on number 19 Rosefield Street, caved in the rear section of the tenement. The Forbes family were among 10 persons trapped on the precipices which remained of the upper floors. John Forbes received a slight injury when a ladder pushed up by an eager volunteer struck him on the nose! The family's six-year-old daughter Jean was later commended for her patience and bravery by John Beat, the head warden. The seventh bomb struck the electricity sub station at Forest Park Place, only narrowly missing the Forest Park cinema, in which 250 people were watching *The Ghost Comes Home* starring Ann Rutherford and Frank Morgan. They felt the shock of the explosion as it lifted the roof off and caused a side wall to collapse. The audience vacated the building in an orderly manner after some minutes of community singing in the dark. The final bomb struck the Queen Victoria works in Brook Street. The only person in the vicinity, a watchman, 67-year-old Thomas Scott, sustained minor cuts and bruises, having been virtually buried in debris. When the all-clear sounded at 9.42pm, repairs began. Gas, water, electricity and telephone lines had been disrupted, although the Dundee Rep continued their performance by candlelight. Later that night, bombs were dropped at Monifieth Grange and Glamis but no more in Dundee.

The huge unexploded bomb in the Arbroath Road was buried at least 20ft down in the earth under tarmac. It took a week's digging to get ropes around it. A crane, driven by a Corporation employee named Andrew Scott, gingerly extracted it and loaded it onto a trailer. Very slowly it was driven north to the Sidlaws and detonated in a controlled explosion which could be heard back in Dundee.

There were other air raids. On 12 February 1941, a Junkers 88 crashed into Cunmont Hill, Monikie, and on 13 March over 100 heavy bombers passed over the Law heading for Clydebank. On 16 March, six bombs were jettisoned by homeward-bound bombers over Tealing, and on 22 March five were jettisoned in the river. On 7 April, at 3.05pm, a 250kg bomb was dropped on Baldovan House, Emmock Road. The only other significant air raid occurred on 2 November 1941 when a bomb was dropped over the Linlathen housing scheme. No one was injured. There were no further attacks on the city for two years, although many German planes were heard raiding the coast of Angus and Fife and there was considerable activity at the mouth of the estuary, including the dropping of mines in the Tay, something which occurred throughout the war. A fourth civilian death occurred on 5 May 1941 when a 24-year-old policeman, PC Robert Stirrat, came across one of these mines on the foreshore at Broughty Ferry, near the bottom of Fisher Street, and attempted to secure it. It exploded and killed him instantly. (For details of Dundee's war dead, see *Appendix, Figure 1*)

The raid in 1943 did not involve bombs. Instead, on 24 April a Luftwaffe pilot swooped low over the Hilltown, opened fire with his machine guns and continued firing in bursts down to Victoria Road. Miraculously, there were no

The fifth bomb on 5 November 1940 was a direct hit on 19 Rosefield Street. Although there were 40 people in the building at the time, only one, Mrs Mary Laing, was killed. (Evening Telegraph, Dundee)

injuries. On 22 April 1944, at 10pm, a plane appeared above the High Street. This had been noted by radar and spotting teams as a 'friendly' since there was a military parade taking place in the High Street. The plane opened fire with machine guns in the High Street and City Square and over the harbour then on to Broughty Ferry, firing intermittent bursts. Again, unbelievably, there was not a single injury.

When the all clear sounded at 4.48pm on 15 September 1944, the 132nd red alert of the war, it proved to be the final time sirens were heard in the city. On 16 May 1945, Dundonians were treated to the bizarre spectacle of a German submarine, *U-2326*, sailing up the Tay and surrendering to a crowd of several hundred at Eastern Wharf. The Germans were treated courteously after a formal surrender ceremony aboard the *Unicorn* (which had been renamed HMS *Cressy*). For many, this was their first sighting of an actual German.

On The Home Front

Life on the home front involved long working hours and a constant struggle to get enough to eat and keep warm. It was an existence governed by ration books, identity cards and the need to 'make do and mend'. There were curtailments, curfews and petty restrictions on many aspects of normal life. For many there was anxiety about family members in the services. But not every one was imbued with the spirit of camaraderie to an equal extent. There was early resistance to blackout – several people were fined and one woman was even jailed for 10 days for refusing to cover her lights. She barricaded herself in her house, fighting with the police who remonstrated with her. Nor was it confined to the working class. The Duke of Strathmore refused to camouflage his historic whitewashed cottages at Glamis. Wartime shortages added to deepening poverty, family dislocation and an inflated crime rate. The state's provision was niggardly. The subsistence payments afforded to servicemen's dependents were barely enough to live on and a sense of class-based grievance remained despite the propaganda of national unity. In Dundee housing conditions were worse than elsewhere, except Glasgow, although the Beechwood scheme completed just before the war was of a remarkably high standard. The public's health was affected by the war. A diptheria epidemic swept the city in January 1941. Within weeks there were 188 notified cases, 10 times the normal rate. All 20,000 children in Dundee were finally immunised but it was the blackout and poor diet which had created the conditions that let diptheria and other illnesses such as measles, mumps and chickenpox thrive. Infant mortality rates rose to 6.7 percent.

At New Year in 1941, there was a serious shortage of alcohol. Many pointed to the massive stocks in bonded warehouses in the Seagate. The *Sunday Post* highlighted this – for different reasons – in a feature 'The Blue Light' which called for dispersal of the highly flammable whisky to safer depositories. Tom Johnston, as Regional Controller of Civil Defence, had a meeting with D.C.

Thomson on the matter. The publisher learned that the bonded whisky was being used as currency to trade for US arms. But lack of alcohol was a serious risk to public order and it was remedied by an ever-increasing amount of dilution so that, it was soon remarked, you had to drink 10 times as much to achieve similar intoxication as before the war. Nonetheless, drunkenness increased by 50 percent in the first few months of 1940. The ever-vigilant Church of Scotland tried to get the pubs to close by blackout time and, even as late as 1942, tried to prevent military and civil defence activity on Sundays.

With families divided due to military service, children were running wild. The chief constable, surveying a huge rise in juvenile crime and truancy, concluded in December 1940 that 'the youth of Dundee are getting wickeder and wickeder.' Attempts were made to involve them in socially useful pursuits such as fire-watching and the salvage scheme – 'Junk To Beat Jerry' – but wartime was a time of great excitement for school-age children, with schools often closing early and the authorities over-stretched and unable to curtail their wayward activities.

There was so much council business that the bailies awarded themselves increased expenses and free travel vouchers on the trams and buses. The air raids of 4 and 5 November 1940 had rendered 24 families homeless and the Corporation expended considerable hot air on the problem, as they did over the question of traffic lights and how to make them conform to blackout regulations. Should the lights have disks or tape over the bulb and if so, how would they operate during daylight hours? There were debates about the junction of Commercial Street, High Street and Murraygate – known as 'Suicide Corner' – where even with the wings of all vehicles painted white to render them just slightly visible, and with the regulation-sized slit of light appearing from the taped-up headlights, it was dangerous to walk after blackout. In early October 1940 this meant between the hours of 7.13pm and 6.50am.

Dundee's inaugural Food Week attracted large audiences to the Marryat Hall on 1 October 1940 to cookery demonstrations organised by the Ministry of Food. 'Waste Not, Want Not' was the motto. Lord Provost John Phin admitted that 'Dundee had been in the habit of feeding very largely from a tin can.' The Corporation noted that few had come forward to claim permits for free or cheap milk under the National Milk Scheme. Fifteen thousand were eligible in the city yet only 10 percent had taken up the offer in 1940. Only 15 percent of mothers and children and only 8 percent of expectant mothers had done so. Gradually this changed as rationing became more rigorously applied. The organisers of Food Week tried hard to extol the virtues of vegetables and the delights of sugarless and eggless cake, beetroot buns and rice pudding with milk substitute and suet to save margarine. The question of food rationing was a constant source of public anger throughout the war and there was particular fury over the question of eggs. Fresh eggs were collected from Angus and Perthshire farms and distributed by quota with rations of powdered egg. But the centralisation of supply and distribution proved such an inflexible system that it couldn't differentiate between a fresh egg and one which had gone off.

The Corporation and the Chamber of Commerce made various half-hearted efforts to investigate rumours of black-market activities, particularly concerning tomatoes, but there seems little evidence of anyone being prosecuted, which probably means that the activity was rife. An odd circumstance reported to Dundee Corporation from the Baths Committee was the loss of 928 towels in one year – a record. Dundee Corporation towels had been observed 'decorating the banks of the Nile,' having presumably been 'borrowed' by soldiers on home leave.

Women were to the fore on the home front as conductors on trams and brickie's labourers. Many continued to work in the jute industry, which had switched to the mass production of sandbags, then when demand fell, they worked in munitions. Valentines' factory converted to ammunition manufacture.

However, mainly because of its location, Dundee did not get its full share of war work. Unemployment remained high, at 6 percent (four times the national average), until August 1942. Instead of Dundee being assigned more war work, it was decided to draft Dundee workers, mainly young women, who were regarded as rootless and therefore expendable, to English factories. The social cost of this for the women concerned or the community was barely considered. Thirteen hundred were sent, of whom less than half were volunteers and some never returned to Dundee. This boosted the nascent Scottish National Party branch in Dundee which campaigned on the issue, as did Dundee's Chamber of Commerce. 'It would appear to be the policy of the government to drain Scotland of all its best labour to the advantage of the English manufacturers and affecting the output of munitions in Scotland,' wrote T.H.D. Bonar, president of the Dundee Chamber. He pointed out that some 80 percent of the female trainees at the Victoria Road school were being sent south. For him, perhaps, this was purely an economic matter. An official deputation sent to Ernest Bevin, the Minister of Labour, included Lord Provost Garnet Wilson. Joined at Westminster by MPs Dingle Foot and Florence Horsbrugh, it was successful in persuading Bevin to call off the repatriation scheme.

> Garnet Wilson was born in 1885 and educated at Cupar, transferring to Dundee High School at the age of 15. He worked in his father's famous drapery business, G.L. Wilson's 'The Corner' and after eight years on the Corporation as a Liberal councillor dealing with education and transport matters, was the surprise choice for Lord Provost when John Phin, who had been appointed District Civil Defence Commissioner, stood down in November 1940. It was unprecedented promotion given his relative inexperience. 'You're new!' remarked George VI on his arrival at Tay Bridge station. Garnet Wilson proved highly effective and popular and held the post until the elections of November 1946. He was also influential in attempts to bring new industry to Dundee after the war. He was later knighted and received an honorary degree from Queen's College.

Churchill's government had acted with brutal swiftness at the outbreak of war to round up the 404 persons in Dundee on the Aliens Register, including 20 Germans and 229 Italians. On 11 June 1940, 100 of the non-naturalised Italians were shipped off to internment camps in the Isle of Man while a further 180 were summarily told to leave the city, which had become a 'protected area'. Many Italian families had sons or daughters serving in the armed forces. But if they did not suffer persecution, they were not treated with the same warmth as the Poles and French who arrived in Dundee to be billeted with Dundee families. The 'Gallant Poles' made a big impact, especially on the women, with their politeness and smart uniforms. But there was a subtler form of racism at work. The King George and Queen Elizabeth Club opened its doors at 21 Reform Street as a club for officers, but there was controversy when it was discovered to be refusing admission to Poles, Norwegians, Dutch and other non-British officers.

Certainly, these sailors and military personnel could enjoy the other social attractions of Dundee, particularly the dance halls, pubs and cafés. The great dance boom had waned in the thirties. The ice rink on the Kingsway, which opened in 1934, was a potent rival attraction, particularly with the American-style glamour of the ice-hockey team. In 1937, the Palais de Danse competed against rival attractions by opening an extension. A new ballroom, the Locarno, opened in Lochee Road. The Duncans, founders of the Palais, opened the Empress Ballroom and Andy Lothian, bandleader at the Palais, became its owner and kept the ballroom going. There was, of course, the Chalet on Broughty Ferry Esplanade and several other smaller ballrooms, including the West End Palais ('Robies') and the Progress Hall on the Hilltown, notorious for

An interior view of the Palais, Tay Street, just before the war. (The Courier, Dundee)

its brawls. Drink and the presence of many uniformed men of different nationalities led to frequent brawls. Cinemas also boomed. The Caird Hall was converted to a cinema to cope with the demand. *Gone With The Wind* played to full houses there for four weeks in 1941. Drama was also popular. Richard Todd was one of the minor actors in the cast in the Rep in Nicoll Street. Amateur opera also boomed and there were many charity concerts.

The churches were dismayed at the change in behaviour of young and not so young women in the absence of their fathers, brothers, husbands and boyfriends. There was criticism of the excessive drinking, bold behaviour and the new jazz music favoured by service personnel and younger set. But for most Dundonians, life was long working hours in factories booming with 'music while you work' over tannoys. This was not merely entertainment. Sometimes it was essential to keep workers awake. 'The dancing' and a fast and free social life seemed to be required compensations for the tedium of war on the home front.

One of Dundee's proudest moments in the war came with 'War Weapons Week'. This soon became a keen competition with other cities, notably Aberdeen. The event opened with a display in City Square which included a Messerschmidt 109 which had been shot down (and was the worse for wear), a Bren gun and a genuine green German parachute. These sad artefacts drew huge crowds. Donations came forward. Within two days, £74,000 had been contributed. The Dundee total broke British records, reaching £3,001,453 4s 7d, of which £595,628 4s 7d was from small investors, or £3 12s 7d per head, which was by far the greatest of all UK cities. The grand total from both categories was beaten only by Edinburgh and London, both of which had much greater resources to draw on. The congratulations of the Chancellor of

Two Luftwaffe airmen are marched along Bell Street to be taken into custody. The rear guard is Robert McDonald, grandfather of Lord Provost Tom McDonald. (Evening Telegraph, Dundee)

the Exchequer were sent north; 'the man and woman in the street of no other city can compare with those of Dundee in their financial support for the national cause.' There was an unsavoury spat with Aberdeen, which accused Dundee of including the Angus figures, which was not the case. Dundee again broke records in 1942 with its contributions to 'Warship Week' – a total of £3,782,775. Dundonians also donated to the 'Aid to Russia' shop in the High Street and delivered their parcels to the POW Appeal Fund Depot in Yeaman Shore, which sent a total of some 142,000 parcels to Germany.

The king and queen spent three and a half hours in Dundee on 1 March 1941, greeting a crowd estimated at 20,000 in City Square and with Tom Johnson, now Secretary of State for Scotland, touring the Ashton Jute Works, the Blackness Foundry and the naval units. Other prominent leaders Clement Atlee, Herbert Morrison, Stafford Cripps and Field-Marshall Wavell visited the city – but there was one notable absentee – Winston Churchill. The prime minister had vowed never again to set foot in Dundee after the ignominy of his defeat at the hands of Neddy Scrimgeour in 1922 – and he kept to his promise.

Celebrations And New Horizons

A jubilant crowd of 50,000 crammed into the City Square to celebrate VJ day in August 1945, as they had done in May for VE day. The celebrations went

Celebrations in the City Square on VE day, May 1945. (The Courier, Dundee)

Dancing in City Square to the music of the City of Dundee Pipe Band. VJ day celebrations, August 1945. (Evening Telegraph, Dundee)

on well into the night and the front of the Caird Hall was lit with floodlights – a welcome sight after nearly five years of the blackout. If you knew where to go, free beer was on offer and there were many private parties. Only one week later, Dundee held its first ever Civic Week, with shows, entertainment and a boxing contest.

Highland dancers draw the crowds as part of VJ day celebrations. (The Courier, Dundee)

In the general election of July 1945 Dingle Foot, the Liberal who had represented the city since 1935, and the redoubtable Conservative Florence Horsbrugh were defeated by Socialist candidates Tom Cook and John Strachey. A feature of the election was the sheer number of previously unregistered electors, 28,000 of them, mainly service personnel, who voted by special airmail 'coupon'. Arthur Donaldson, a Scottish Nationalist (and pacifist) standing for the first time, gained 7,000 votes and lost his deposit, although in Motherwell the SNP gained their first MP. The Socialists won the municipal elections in November 1946 and Archibald Powrie replaced Garnet Wilson as Lord Provost but died in January 1949. John Adamson, installed in February, spent only three months in office because the moderates' success at the polls in May resulted in Richard Fenton being sworn in. Within a year, Dundee had had three Lord Provosts.

For most people in Dundee, there was social dislocation as families strove to make the best of things. A baby boom was well under way, but 1947 was also to be the peak year for divorces. The war created significant social change, raised aspirations and changed perceptions of social class. For children, the school leaving age was raised to 15 and things got back to normal after the exciting war years. It was estimated that 5,000 Dundee soldiers had married during the war and this included many Polish and some French soldiers. The Corporation had taken the step in April 1944 of ordering 3,000 'Portal' houses. This had been opposed by the Socialist group. Councillor Harry Hird

Florence Horsbrugh, Dundee's only Conservative MP, was defeated in the general election of August 1945, along with the Liberal, Dingle Foot. (The Courier, Dundee)

Wing-Commander Edward John St Loe Strachey was a political animal and something of an intellectual. He had previously dallied with the Conservatives, the ILP, the Communist Party – a legacy of which was a serious crisis later in his career when his friendship with Klaus Fuchs, the German communist convicted of passing Britain's nuclear secrets to the Russians, was revealed – and he had even flirted briefly with Oswald Mosley's New Party. He was appointed to the post of Food Minister in 1945. This was a poisoned chalice and when he introduced bread rationing for the first time in Britain he became very unpopular. Bread rationing was one of the reasons for the defeat of the Labour Government in the elections of 1950 and 1951. Strachey was involved in many stormy meetings in Dundee about bread. He was particularly harassed by the Dundee branch of the Scottish Housewives Association. One of his books, *The End Of Empire,* published in 1959, contended that Britain was better off without its empire, but he believed that it had had beneficial as well as iniquitous effects. Strachey remained a Dundee MP until his death in 1963.

Dundee's new socialist MPs; Tom Cook (on left) and John Strachey with Mrs Strachey leaving the Court House, August 1945. (Evening Telegraph, Dundee)

John Strachey MP meets representatives of the Dundee Branch of the Scottish Housewives Association in March 1949. (Evening Telegraph, Dundee)

described these prefabs constructed of tin alloy as 'an insult to the working class'. To Hird, they were 'super bully cans' worse than the other types of prefabs available. The first prefabs had appeared at Seabraes in 1943, but whereas in England they were replacing bombed-out homes, in Dundee they were used as a cheap housing solution. The Corporation could not afford to build another Beechwood and with the passing of the Temporary Accomodation Act in 1944, more prefabs were built at Douglas & Angus, Camperdown and at Mains of Fintry. But the extent of the crisis was not yet clear. It was estimated that up to 12,000 service personnel had yet to return to the city.

Concern about the unemployed – there were about 3,500 unemployed in Dundee at this time, mainly demobbed servicemen – led to the holding of a conference in the city in 1945. The housing situation in Dundee was acute and there was a protracted debate about the future of Dundee's largest mansion, Castleroy. The 100-roomed residence built by Gilroy, the jute owner, was offered to the city but initially refused due to the costs of maintenance. Plans evolved for it to become a rest home. It was estimated that some of the 2,000 OAPs in the city might pay 15 shillings per week to stay there, thus freeing

their own homes for younger tenants. In the meantime, squatters moved in and as the Corporation debated endlessly, soon there was no alternative but demolition.

Princess Elizabeth opened the 400-acre Camperdown Park in 1946. Dressed in a tailored oatmeal-coloured coat and pink hat, she was making her first public appearance in Scotland. She planted a beech seedling at Camperdown House and made a speech in which she recalled her childhood days at Glamis. 'A trip to Dundee was always enjoyed,' she recalled. Her youth and freshness

seemed to personify the new post-war era. In April 1948 Bernard Street, a cul-de-sac off Hawkhill, was packed with 1,000 Dundonians celebrating the royal wedding. They danced eightsome reels beneath bunting hung with portraits of king and queen, and Mrs Margaret Shepherd, one of the organisers, said: 'We do things in style. The papers said we were the best street in Britain. We washed the street for the occasion.'

The Labour Government had appointed Harold Wilson as President of the Board of Trade. Senior figures of the jute industry invited him to a meeting at the Chamber of Commerce on 16 June 1948 to discuss the post-war future for the industry. But 50 members of the Dundee Scottish Housewives Association seized the opportunity to demonstrate against household linen rationing. They massed under Queen Victoria's statue in Albert Square with home-made banners and a 31,000 signature petition. However, Wilson was let into the Chamber of Commerce building by the Meadowside door and evaded them.

There was more drama in December 1948 involving a Tay ferry, the Caledon-built *Sir William High*. Leaving Newport pier in fog she overshot Craig Pier on the north bank, went astern to make another run and became trapped on rock by an ebb of the tide. The boat was just 100 yards from the western wharf and the passengers were able to shout to the pierman. The *Mona* lifeboat from Broughty Ferry tried to locate its winking red light, invisible from even 20 yards away. The 60 or so passengers did not think they

The Sir William High, *the only 'Fifie' without radar, was scheduled to be replaced when the accident occurred in thick fog in December 1948.* (Evening Telegraph, Dundee)

Gracie Fields with her friend Mrs Mary Davey, on a shopping expedition after her concerts in Dundee, May 1949. Her popularity led to such a demand for tickets at Methven Simpsons' music shop in Reform Street that a second concert was added – and sold out within two days. (Evening Telegraph, Dundee)

were in any danger and engaged in light-hearted banter, but the harbour officials, aware there were two hours of ebb tide ahead, feared the ship might take a sudden list. Anything could happen if her cargo, mainly vehicles and a small bus, started to move. The ferry skipper fired off a couple of rockets to help the *Mona*'s coxswain find her, but there was so little water that the lifeboat had to berth directly astern. Women and children were taken off first and landed at Camperdown lockway, a mile east of their original destination. The lifeboat returned for the remainder of the passengers and crew. The 'Fifie' floated unassisted on the flood tide the next morning. She had sustained a lot of damage to her hull and was out of service for several weeks during which she had radar fitted. It could have ended in tragedy.

The *Glasgow Herald* of 10 January 1949 reported that the simmering issue of the status of Queen's College, Dundee, was to be tested with an inquiry. St Andrews was generally the home of classics, while Dundee was the centre for

engineering, although sciences, modern languages and the medical school were shared. The medical school was at the core of the dispute. The new principal of Queen's College, Major-General D.N. Wimberley, prepared a report in 1946. Wimberley was not a secessionist. He mainly wanted the college to expand and take a greater role within Dundee. One result of the controversy, reported the *Herald*, 'is that it has made Dundonians for the first time 'university-minded'.

The end of clothing rationing in March 1949 was marked with celebration sales in the city's department stores. Sweets, normally obtainable only by coupons, were distributed free in some Dundee schools by drawing lots when a gift of 7,000 pounds of sugar was received from the people of Havana in April. Confectioners complained to the Ministry of Food that the quota system was moribund and called for an end to sugar rationing.

Dundonians were reading more books. The *Evening Telegraph* of 26 April 1949 reported the plea of Mr J. Duncan Dundas, librarian, to move facilities from the Albert Institute to a modern new building in the Overgate adjoining the city churches. Accomodation was too cramped and the cellars were crammed with books at risk from frequent floods.

In August 1949, the 50 staff and 1,500 pupils of the Morgan Academy celebrated its diamond jubilee year. Plans for a new hospital and medical school were announced. Optimism and reconstruction were the keynotes as

The Royal Highland Show held at Riverside Park in June 1949 attracted a record attendance of 163,917 spectators. (The Courier, Dundee)

the decade came to an end. The Scottish National Party, which had formed branches in West End, Downfield and Dundee East, planned a meeting in the Caird Hall and an all-party committee, chaired by Garnet Wilson, of the Scottish Covenant movement was set up calling for Scottish Home Rule. The Central Library agreed to provide facilities for the public to sign it. The total number of signatories was to reach nearly two million. That too was a marker for the future, a sign of optimism and aspiration.

CHAPTER 2

An End to Austerity

The Housing Explosion

There were nearly 21,000 names on the City Factor's list in February 1951 and housing was the immediate, overriding priority. In 1945 the first tenants had moved in to the Kirkton Estate and by the new decade there were 1,400 tenants there, paying an average rent of 15s 10d per week. Gradually they became aware that there were no local amenities. In December 1951, Kirkton Tenants' Association was formed and soon had over 800 paying members. The Corporation was forced to act. A temporary playing field was created in Derwent Avenue. There were more basic problems with the houses built in Coniston Terrace in 1945. Due to steel shortages, spares for cookers were

Panoramic view of Camperdown housing estate, early 1950s. Note the sheep grazing in the fields! (The Courier, Dundee)

unavailable so tenants were forced to resort to other means of cooking their food. Since the Corporation could not provide a community centre, the tenants raised money themselves. They held social functions in West March Hall to raise the deposit of £50 on a Nissen hut to be a social club, in which they planned to hold evening classes and lectures for young people. They also planned a bowling green.

In 1954, following the Government's withdrawal of building restrictions, Bett Brothers decided to erect two traditional-type villas in Sherbrook Street, Downfield. They wanted to find out if the public would be interested in buying houses. The two villas were readily sold and the company built 12 more on the same site. Thereafter a variety of bungalow and villa types were offered among 170 built at Sherbrook Street. Then Betts located a patch of almost derelict land at Abertay Street, Barnhill. Houses were built in Backhill Road in Balgay, at Burn Street, Downfield, at Claypotts and in Windsor Street. A total of over 400 private dwellings were built with almost two miles of new streets completed by Betts over two years. House prices ranged from a three-apartment bungalow costing £1,750 to a five-apartment villa for £2,675. Betts also acquired land in Monifieth.

Since the 'baby boomers' were approaching school age, work was underway on a 29-acre site building Kirkton's new £250,000 school, the largest to be built in Scotland since the war. Truscon Ltd, with Charles Gray as subcontractor, constructed the school from precast reinforced concrete, a fairly innovative method for Britain at that time. Linlathen primary and infants schools were converted, and a new classroom block was built to create a 'bargain' school which opened in August 1958 having cost only £60,000.

In April 1959, Charles Gray unveiled plans for a Buttar's Loan shopping centre to form a hub between Camperdown, Dryburgh and proposed new schemes in South Road and Menzieshill. This was to serve the 13,000 council tenants in the area and the additional 14,000 expected when the new schemes were completed. This was housing on a grand scale. A note of caution was expressed by the town clerk, Robert Lyle. He considered that it was time 'to call a halt to these housing estates… unless they are to have the facilities of halls, libraries, medical, shopping, recreational, social and other amenities.' The urgent need to rehouse people living in slums and overcrowded conditions had 'largely been addressed,' he believed. The new estates had populations similar to the small burghs (Arbroath 20,000, Montrose 11,000, Forfar 10,000), but without their amenities. 'New housing is something more than just new homes and dormitories with travelling facilities to and from work,' Lyle believed. The authorities had, in his words, 'so far ignored most if not all of these considerations in their zeal for new homes.' It was a popular view and the local press interviewed residents who by and large agreed, but these issues were not considered important enough by the Housing Division to halt the pace of construction of the new scheme at Menzieshill. Throughout the 1950s the Corporation was driven by its perception of the acute housing shortage and its priority was to build houses as quickly and cheaply as possible.

The Expansion of Industry

The other main concern of local politicians at the end of the war was the need for new industry. The Distribution of Industry Bill of 1945 had been framed to promote the traditional depressed areas. Dundee was not one of these but was belatedly included as a new 'grey area' in the Act. The Scottish Home Department commented that 'while one fifth of Dundee's working population is still engaged in jute, Dundee's chief need is for diversification of industry.' Capital projects with a total estimated cost of £500,000 were given an early start. A spur to industrial development was the construction of the ring-road, the Kingsway.

The future of jute was uncertain. There was small-scale expansion; a new jute factory, the Taybank Works was built in 1949, and there was a labour shortage which resulted in several hundred workers from Pakistan arriving to work in the mills. The prosperity of Dundee still largely depended on jute until the mid-1960s, but the industry was predicated on the continuation of the

View of Shore Terrace looking westwards, September 1951. (The Courier, Dundee)

Unloading a jute liner; a busy scene at King George Wharf in 1952. Jute had declined from 37 manufacturers in 1945 to 22, but was to remain Dundee's single largest employer until 1966. (Evening Telegraph, Dundee)

Shore porter David Kennedy of Ballantrae Place unloading jute at Eastern Wharf in 1958. (Evening Telegraph, Dundee)

wartime Jute Control Order. The President of the Board of Trade, as supreme Jute Controller, bought all the processed jute from India to prevent it being sold at its economic price. In 1957 the degree of protection was reduced from 40 percent to 30 percent. The Dundee manufacturers got a shock. They had spent £11 million modernising and thought they were immune, but jute control survived until 1969.

Lord Provost Garnet Wilson cut the sod at Camperdown on behalf of the Scottish Industrial Estates Corporation on 15 April 1946 and was influential in attracting NCR (manufacturing) Ltd and a light engineering company from Dayton, Ohio, to the city as well as the overall manufacturers, Hamilton Carharrt. Valentines' greetings card factory – the largest in Britain – had moved to the Kingsway in 1937 and James Keiller & Son relocated to Lammerton Terrace.

Gradually, the industrial estate took shape. Despite shortages of labour and materials, eight factories were under construction by the end of the first year, and Ministry of Works land at King's Cross was incorporated to bring the total up to half a million square feet on almost 90 acres.

Meanwhile, over in the east, an industrial estate was formed to incorporate the watchmaking factory of UK Time Co. Ltd, which housed nearly 1,000 employees and the Astral factory, formerly a jute works at Milton of Craigie. In September 1959 when Astral (renamed Morphy Richards) needed more space, 24 acres were acquired at Gourdie. Their claim was that they could produce a spin-dryer every two and a half minutes. Astral had started in

An exterior view of the NCR factory, one of the earliest arrivals in the Dundee industrial estate in 1946. (The Courier, Dundee)

Dundee with 40 workers in 1947 but now employed 1,000 and planned to build a new factory within two years to produce refrigerators. This was to employ up to 800 people, with a build up over two years to 1,200, and establish Dundee as a leading centre for mass production of domestic electrical appliances. A third industrial estate was built on a 47-acre piece of land at Wester Gourdie.

The assembly lines at NCR hard at work constructing cash registers, 1953. (The Courier, Dundee)

The testing department at the Astral factory, Milton of Craigie, September 1959. Astral had started in Dundee in 1947 with 40 workers but now employed 1,000. (The Courier, Dundee)

By 1953, Dundee was thriving with a diversity of old and new industries. Despite long-term anxieties over textiles, there were 22 jute manufacturers, three linen and flax manufacturers, the Dundee Linoleum Company and three manufacturers of textile equipment and machinery in the city. The textiles sector was boosted by the floods of February 1953 when orders were placed for 20 million sandbags. Dundee workers worked in shifts around the clock and at weekends. Appeals were issued for former machinists and special buses were deployed. There was particular interest in an unburstable sack being developed at Sidlaw Industries which incorporated polypropylene. The order was completed together with orders for 3.5 million more. Dundee's 18,000 jute workers were given Christmas Day off in 1956 in addition to the two days at New Year. An increasing range of jute products were being produced and tufted carpet backing and polypropylene were major growth areas. Sidlaw Industries, Low & Bonar and Tay Textiles between them accounted for two-thirds of UK production by the mid-1970s.

The Hart-Ashworth Company on the Kingsway was the only large felt manufacturing firm in Scotland. In 1960, the factory began production of a range of felt motor scooter and motorcycle helmets, which, it was claimed, were safer than glass fibre. The L.S. Mayer factory mass-produced imitation leather bags and James Keiller's preserves and confectionery factory attracted worldwide success. Burndept, one of the earliest newcomers to the industrial estate in 1946, had begun as Vidor Batteries, which relocated from Kent to a Dundee jute mill in 1941 to escape German bombing. After five years making a range of dry-cell batteries they were successful enough to move to the Kingsway, boosting their number of employees to 1,000 and becoming the largest dry battery producer in Western Europe.

Remploy, a trading organisation set up by and responsible to the Ministry of Labour, had started in Methven Street, Lochee, in 1948 with 10 disabled employees. Its workers, half of whom were disabled ex-servicemen, made a wide range of products from bedroom suites to brushes, tents and haversacks.

Bonar Long was one of the earliest factories on the industrial estate and

The hat brushing machine at the Hart-Ashworth factory, 1959. A member of the Luton-based Hubbard group, the factory produced three million hoods every year and boasted that 'every second hat began its life in Dundee'. (The Courier, Dundee)

The Baron Kilmarnock, launched from the Caledon yard on 16 March 1953, was the largest ship built on the Tay. (The Courier, Dundee)

rapidly expanded into a large export business with 500 employees. In November 1958 the firm built its fifth extension, a 55,000sq ft hall for the manufacture of electrical transformer equipment for power stations. Believed to be the first built in Britain with reinforced concrete instead of steel and brick, the building housed a travelling crane, the largest in Scotland at 100 tons, with a 60-foot span.

With industry booming, strikes became an infrequent occurrence, but where they occurred they were generally successful. The AEU organised a strike for its maintenance men and mechanics in the jute mills in January 1953. With 97 percent of the members taking part their demands were met in full.

The Calcdon yard was booming. The largest Tay-built tanker, the 13,500-ton *Aida,* left Dundee for trials in North Sea, built for Olof Wallenius of Stockholm. Her title was lost just one week later when her sister, the *Sunnaas,* built for Iver Bugge of Norway, was launched from the yard. Caledon had orders for even larger tankers of 16,500 and 18,000 tonnes. In the docks, William Briggs & Co. were producing a large range of bitumen products, roofing felts, protective paints and tarmac and another local company, BX Plastics, was also involved in the chemicals sector. In the first half of the 1950s, Dundee dock workers often unloaded 50 different liners from jute ports, with

Workers pour from the Caledon yard gates in 1955. (Evening Telegraph, Dundee)

A view of the underused Earl Grey Dock in 1956. Apart from HMS Cressy *(better know as HM Frigate* Unicorn*) and HMS* Jewel *of the navy's 'mothball' fleet, these century-old docks were given over to the sandboat fleet and, in autumn and winter, sprat yawls. (Evening Telegraph, Dundee)*

ever-larger cargoes and other tankers bringing phosphates and materials for the cement trades.

Other parts of the docks were redundant. Some of the oldest harbour trades had declined. Local coasters carrying coal, salt, slates and firewood, the windjammers, the cattle trade from Canada and Ireland, Canadian flour – all had ceased. There were no more imports of cottonseed from Egypt and India, linseed from India and the river Plate, copper ore from Spain, phosphates from Mediterranean and Pacific, pitch-pine from British Colombia or crushed oyster shells (for poultry feed) from America.

A new 'Fifie', the *Scotscraig,* was launched in May 1951. The name had been on Dundee shipping registers for 140 years but in July 1954, the last of Dundee's trawling fleet, the *Fraser Fenton,* was sold. Though Dundee was never a serious rival of Aberdeen, it had been able to meet the local enthusiasm for fresh haddock and export whiting to Glasgow and northern England. The exhaustion of the nearby haddock spawning grounds which could be fished over three or four days and the soaring cost of bunker coal made it unprofitable. The *Fraser Fenton* was transferred to the port of Aberdeen.

By 1957 visitors could see a panorama of nine modern ships stretching from the Queen Elizabeth Wharf to Caledon's east jetty. These ships included the Caledon-built Blue Star liner *Canadian Star*. In 1959, the Tay ferries were deriving 70 percent of their income from vehicular traffic. Steam engines had begun to disappear. In the Dundee area, diesel trains had started taking over from steam on passenger services. Firstly, a three-month training programme was required. In 12 weeks, 85 drivers were trained on diesels, 55 from the Dundee depot. An *Evening Telegraph* reporter went on assignment with a driver on the run from Dundee to Perth and was favourably impressed by the lack of smoke smuts, pieces of coal or acrid smell of smoke. There were no jolts or bangs and very little swaying. 'No doubt about which I prefer to travel in,' he commented.

Despite the post-war boom, there was still concern about Dundee's 5.2 percent unemployment rate. This was better than many other parts of Scotland but was nevertheless a worrying rise in a booming local economy. Some of it was temporary, particularly in the building trades, which suffered from the vagaries of demand. An unemployed man with a wife and two children received 'dole' money of £5 per week, while the lowest male wage, earned by a coalman, was £8 per week, so unemployment was something most families dreaded.

A Better Quality of Life

The early post-war years brought huge improvements to the lives of ordinary Dundonians. One of the most important was the introduction of universal old-age

The jute liner, City of Dundee, *in 1954 – another product of the Caledon yard. (The Courier, Dundee)*

Mr Tommy Herd lines up hackles on a finished stave in the inspection department of William R. Stewart & Sons, Hacklemakers, 1956. (The Courier, Dundee)

The Campania, Festival *of Britain ship, was a borrowed aircraft carrier. The 'shining colossus of the sea' slid up the Tay in bright sunshine on 16 May 1951 and remained for 10 days at King George Wharf as a floating exhibition. Special arrangements were made for public buses and parking. (The Courier, Dundee)*

pensions in May 1951. This was part of the Beveridge Report, introduced by Atlee's Government for men of 65 and women of 60. Soon after, in February 1952, identity cards were abolished, although rationing lingered on until July 1954 when coupons for meat were abolished.

Dundee's Own exhibition in the Caird Hall in September 1952 featured an early type of aircraft flight simulator. You could sit in the cockpit of a meteor jet fighter and 'fly' at 600mph, watching the runway and scenery on a screen, but on 28 August 1951, the real thing could be seen. A large silver aircraft, the Bristol Brabazon, flew over the centre of the city at a few minutes past noon, banked gracefully and headed south over the Tay. On board as an invited guest was Bailie Ingram, deputising for Lord Provost Fenton, who reported that he had himself already flown several times to the continent. He was effusive about the plane's performance and noted that the Brabazon was capable of a maximum speed of 250mph and had a wingspan of 230ft.

On 19 April 1952, Dundee FC fans travelled by more mundane means to Hampden to see their team play Motherwell in the Scottish Cup final. The crowd, a record gate of 136,274, watched Dundee lose 4-0, but their team won the League Cup in both the 1951–2 and 1952–3 seasons, a rare feat.

Tickets to see Danny Kaye at the Caird Hall on 7 July 1952 were in big demand. It was the only Scottish date of his UK tour. The queue outside Methven Simpson's was four deep up Reform Street and halfway along Bank Street when the shop opened. Shop assistants Mary Farquhar of Strathmartine Road, Arine Swan of St Kilda's Road and railway porter John Prophet of Drumlanrig Drive were first to get tickets, the girls having camped outside the shop with flasks and sandwiches since the early hours.

The entertainer, a 'typical American figure in a smart grey sports jacket with the bottoms of his trousers tucked up at the back,' arrived in the late afternoon of 7 July from Newcastle and stayed two nights at the Royal Hotel. He travelled to St Andrews to play golf and, after lunch in the New Club, played a few more holes then returned to Dundee in his Rolls-Royce on the ferry, evaded the crowd and had a preview of the Caird Hall. He performed a few soft-shoe taps while his agent tinkled the piano in the dark then he retired to the dressing room. 'I don't know about you fellas,' he said, 'but I think I'll sit here until the show begins.' Someone mentioned the noise outside in the City Square from a by-election campaign. They hoped he would make himself heard. Danny Kaye grinned. 'I can holler when I like.'

The concerts were a great success. 'A slim young man with straw-coloured

A view of the frontage of Queen's College, Dundee, from Nethergate, in the early 1950s. A Royal Commission had been appointed in May 1950 to consider the question of higher education at Dundee and its relationship with St Andrews University. (The Courier, Dundee)

hair and an engaging smile [he] held the emotions of over 3,000 in the palm of his hand for an hour and a half...' the local paper reported. The crowd whistled and shouted and stamped. Danny gave several encores then the 6.15pm house poured out one side and the 8.45pm house came in the other. His glorious clowning and singing made the audience's sides sore with laughter. 'It wasn't what he said. It was how he said it,' reported the journalist. During the second show, he dismissed the band, drew a chair over to the microphone and sang a selection of songs from his latest film. Hundreds waited around in the rain to see him off at midnight. Next day, the headline read 'Fans Wouldn't Let Danny Go.'

Almost in the footsteps of Danny Kaye, Bob Hope arrived in Dundee in September and was jostled and cheered by 2,000 mainly teenage fans as he entered Green's Playhouse between his shows. In the pushing and shoving, a glass panel was smashed in the entrance door and the comedian lost a button and was forced to change his suit. A crowd of some 5,000 was waiting for him in the City Square. The Caird Hall shows were sold out and his 75-minute show, mostly without props of any kind, was a ceaseless barrage of laughter at his effortless wisecracks. He came to Dundee every three years, he said, 'for a change of marmalade.' At the end, after three encores, he was reduced to pleading; 'don't you have homes to go to?'

Gracie Fields returned to Dundee and stayed for two nights at the Royal Hotel. She performed on 13 November 1952 and on the day after visited James Hay's antique dealers at 89½ Ann Street, looking for a French dining table. She lunched at the hotel and left for Glasgow on the 3pm train to prepare for her live TV show. She told well-wishers at the station that she had enjoyed her visit to Dundee very much and looked forward to re-turning. She did so, two years later.

American evangelist Billy Graham began his three-month long crusade in Scotland in 1954 and some Dundonians travelled to Glasgow to join his 17,500-strong audiences in the Kelvin Hall. The services were relayed to St Clement's Church in Dundee and his colour film, *Oil Town Texas,* was shown to a packed audience in the Gilfillan Memorial Church. At

'Samuel's' Corner' at the junction of High Street and Reform Street has long been a favourite meeting place, as this picture from the mid-1950s shows. (Evening Telegraph, Dundee)

Firemen battling the protracted blaze aboard the City of Colchester *on 7 March 1952. The jute cargo fire was, according to the chief fire officer 'the most protracted in the history of Dundee harbour... it will be weeks before the last sodden charred bale can be removed.' (The Courier, Dundee)*

American comic Bob Hope relaxing before his show at the Caird Hall in September 1952. Queues waited patiently at Methven Simpsons, Reform Street, to obtain tickets to the shows which were completely sold out. (Evening Telegraph, Dundee)

many rallies held in Dundee churches involving preachers of the Billy Graham team hundreds came forward to be converted. On 12 April 1955, 1,200 attended a relay service in the Steeple church.

One visitor certain to get a rapturous welcome in Dundee was Beniamino Gigli, the world famous Italian tenor. Agents had first attempted to arrange a concert for Gigli in 1946 but the Caird Hall proved unavailable, then in 1947 the singer had influenza and was unable to appear. Gigli finally performed in the Caird Hall, after some postponements and rearranged dates, in October 1950. He returned in March 1953 and again in March 1954. He was about to celebrate his 64th birthday on the day he arrived in the snow and slush at Dundee's West Station in 1954. Some admirers were waiting to welcome him and escort him to the Royal Hotel. He announced that he would 'sing as long as people wanted him'. His concert of 14 songs included arias from *Rigoletto, La Bohème, Tosca* and popular Neopolitan songs like *Torna a Surriento*. The maestro was forced to give 12 encores.

Coronation fever in Bernard Street, a cul-de-sac off the Hawkhill in June 1953. The residents hosted concerts and dances and at night light bulbs lit up the street among 1,200 flags as they vied – and outdid – the rival displays of Balfour Street, Lamb's Lane and Raglan Street to win the accolade of being Dundee's 'Coronation Alley'. (The Courier, Dundee)

In 1952, King George VI died of a heart attack at the age of 56. A heavy smoker, he had been suffering from lung cancer for two years. After the state funeral, the young Princess Elizabeth was crowned queen. The Coronation aroused frenzied excitement and on 2 June 1953, 10,000 watched the ceremony, televised for the first time, on TV screens set up in the Caird Hall.

Frank Sinatra, described on the advertising of the Chalmers Wood Theatrical Agency of Glasgow as 'a top-line American crooner', played two shows back-to-back at the Caird Hall in Dundee on 13 July 1953. Despite the fact that the singer had just won an Academy Award for his part in *From Here To Eternity*, his first show attracted only 600, making the vast Caird Hall look

Dundee's last tram sets out on its final trip from the High Street to Lochee at 11.30pm on 20 October 1956. (The Courier, Dundee)

almost empty. For an hour before the singer appeared, the Billy Tennent Orchestra with vocalists Eva Beynon and Johnny Webb had been warming up the audience. Francis Albert took the poor house in his stride and suggested that those at the back come forward to the dearer seats. He praised the 'wonderful, enthusiastic audience' and the hall acoustics and, although he was suffering from the onset of a cold, turned in a great performance, tilting the microphone up and down, left and right as he sang *September Song, Birth of the Blues, Nancy With The Laughing Face* and *You'll Never Walk Alone*, each received with raptures from the audience. He sang *Ol' Man River* and diverted into a parody; 'Ole man Crosby… he just keeps singing, he never stops singing along…' In all, 13 numbers with a short pause for a cup of tea. 'It's good for the vocal chords I'm told,' he declared. 'But I take it because I like it.' The second house had attracted 1,189 and one of them was Cathie McCabe, a keen Sinatra fan.

Frank Sinatra signs autographs after his shows at the Caird Hall, 13 July 1953. Asked about the relatively poor turnout, the singer shrugged. 'That happens in other cities,' he said. 'What really matters is their response and it was wonderful. I have a very high opinion of Scottish audiences.' (The Courier, Dundee)

Before the show, the singer had put in an appearance at the Open Golf Championship at Carnoustie, chatting to Ben Hogan, who won the tournament that year.

Musical tastes were diversifying and the wartime boom in dance halls had long since dissipated. A new generation was less interested in orchestral dance music. The Dundee Jazz Club had been set up in a building in Parker Street and was the coolest place in town for the duffle-coated followers of 'trad'. The Sunday night sessions attracted some of the greatest names over the years including Chris Barber, the Mick Mulligan Band featuring George Melly on vocals, George Chisholm, Harry Hall, the Bruce Turner Jump Band, Alex Welsh, Terry Lightfoot and Kenny Ball. In 1961, a new jazz club, the Tomb, opened in Nicoll Street.

When J.M. Wallace opened the JM Ballroom in late 1953, it was the new generation he was interested in attracting. Since he was aware of the wildness associated with new music from America, from the outset he laid down strict rules about behaviour, determined to avoid 'roughness'. The gentleman had to hold the girl's right hand but always above waist level. Dancing cheek to cheek was out. 'Certainly there is nothing wrong,' he stated, 'with a man dancing close to his wife or girlfriend. But what if some Smart Alec sees this and

The front of Dundee East Station in December 1958. It closed in 1960. (The Courier, Dundee)

interrupts him at an "excuse-me" dance? He might become offended if she did not dance with him in the same way. Then trouble starts. The appearance of patrons is another thing I am strict about.' 'Murdie' insisted that males without a tie or dressed untidily would not be admitted, and later he barred girls when their skirts were deemed too short. He believed mini-skirts 'encouraged males to act in an un-gentlemanly way.' Wallace's strictness meant that the JM remained a relatively trouble-free venue, despite the growing city-wide problem of gangs. He operated a blacklist of those who turned up drunk and paid doormen to enforce it.

At the Palais, Charlie Coats was the young vocalist with the 12-piece Andy Lothian Band. He had been hired after singing on guest spots on Sunday nights. 'Guest nights' were a hard apprenticeship. If the audience liked the singer, they cheered and the singer sang again, but if the audience did not cheer, your career was over before it had begun. Charlie Coats retired in 1972 at the early age of 43, by which time he reckoned he had launched a thousand dances and sung up to 150 songs a week. 'It was seven nights a week plus two

*The Empress Ballroom
was one of the oldest
remaining dance halls in
the early 1950s and
tended to cater for older
patrons.* (Evening
Telegraph, Dundee)

afternoon sessions. All strict tempo stuff, no jitterbugging,' he recalled. He was expected to be able to sing all the chart hits in the week in which they appeared. One of the most successful evenings was the Ray Ellington Quartet Night on 14 June 1959. Ellington was on top of the charts that week and drew huge crowds, with at least 1,000 managing to get inside.

There are many JM stories, including the tale of the American serviceman, first seen knocking on the front door at 7.30pm, who was told to come back when the venue opened at 8pm. He did so and at 9.30pm was seen in the balcony cafeteria with a girl. At 11pm he left to escort her home and explained on leaving that some of his relatives had been born in Dundee and he had come to see the place. He told Wallace that he was 'mighty glad' he had for he had just met his wife. He said he intended to marry the girl the very next day. Several years later, the couple returned with two children in tow to revisit the place where they had met. There were also tales of a Dundee girl who met an Indian prince at the JM and married him, the visits of celebrities such as Primo Carnera, a world heavyweight boxing champion and the 20 African chiefs,

J. Murdoch Wallace, or 'Murdie', be-spectacled, squat, with his trademark soft hat, cigar and Rolls-Royce Silver Cloud JM9. Aside from his business interests, he stood unsuccessfully for the council many times from the late 1920s onwards on an anti-corruption platform, being strongly influenced by former Prohibitionist MP Neddy Scrimgeour – he was a teetotaller – but also stood for the Socialists and the Progressives and made electoral history by contesting both Broughty Ferry wards at the same election. This led to a new statute prohibiting a candidate from standing in more than one ward simultaneously. He once spent a night in Bell Street cells for refusing to pay a speeding ticket but next morning, rather than be remanded to Barlinnie, he proffered a £100 note and paid the fine, much to the inconvenience of the police, who had to send a man out to the bank to get change. He died in March 1969 aged 65.

some in tribal dress, who caused a commotion on the dance floor. Tuesdays at the ballroom were reserved for the 12–16s, some of the boys dancing in short trousers and girls in ankle socks. Every popular dance in vogue from the twist to disco boogie was practised on the floor of the

J. Murdoch ('Murdie') Wallace was a familiar and convivial figure of the 1950s and '60s. He started out as a baker in the Blackness Road and acquired a shop in the Overgate, a coffee stall in Lindsay Street and the Angus Garage prior to opening the JM Ballroom in late 1953. (Evening Telegraph, Dundee)

Johnny Victory in April 1956 with the vintage Rolls-Royce which had once belonged to Sir Harry Lauder, outside the Palace Theatre. (The Courier, Dundee)

JM with greater or lesser finesse. The floodgates to modernity opened in 1959 – until then no jiving was allowed – when suddenly a jive set was announced to everyone's astonishment.

The phenomenon of 'Teddy boys' had caused alarm enough for the government to set up a commission to investigate it in 1954. Dundee too had its Teddy boys. Since the ballrooms in Dundee refused them entry they were forced to try elsewhere. Large groups sometimes hired buses to take them to Angus towns. These weekend 'invasions' caused considerable trouble. One such convoy of two buses in December 1955 was refused entry in Brechin and then tried various dance halls in Montrose, finally being evicted from the Locarno. 'The drape suiters,' reported the local paper, 'made off, some cursing the management, and – from a safe distance – two of them shouted – "Wait till ya come tae Dundee. We'll cut ya up!"' The Locarno manager reported that 'their language, especially that of the women is shocking. Their type of dress just precipitates trouble...' But his greatest complaint was that 'they are not interested in mixed dancing of the type we provide... only in the modern stuff.'

In the early 1950s there were still punch-ups outside the Progress dance hall in the Hilltown, as there had been during the war, although Dundee also had the reputation of having the tallest police constables in Britain at the time, with an average height of over six feet, the tallest being PC George Wilson, six foot nine inches, not counting the additional height afforded by his blue spiked helmet! Since the average height of a Dundonian male has remained five foot six inches for generations, the police had a distinct advantage in these 'rammies'.

The Empire Cinema in Rosebank Street had a full-house when *Rock Around the Clock* was screened in 1956. Gangs of youths outside, desperate to see the film, or merely intent on causing trouble, burst in through the exit doors and could not be ejected. Some members of the audience started dancing on their seats or jiving in the aisles and it was the same when *The Girl Can't Help It* screened at the Broadway in Arthurstone Terrace and *Don't Knock The Rock* came to the Empire in the following year. Seat-slashing became endemic. Style was everything to the youths who were classified as 'Teds' and the intricate variations of cut, drape, numbers of pockets, shape of seams, collar – whether velvet or cutaway – and, of course, the haircut were crucial. Too often violence was the end result and the worst battles occurred around the dodgems at the Gussie Park carnival when razors and bicycle chains were among the weapons used. A range of coffee bars operated to cater for the different groups such as the Coffee Cup in Albert Street and 40s in Dura Street, with the ever-present jukeboxes.

But not everyone wanted raucous noise. On Sunday 13 February 1955 the City of Dundee Orchestra gave its first public concert in the Gaumont cinema. This was composed of many well-known local players, conducted by James

The Queen at the centenary of Dundee Royal Infirmary, June 1955. (The Courier, Dundee)

Easson. Tickets were priced between 1s 6d and 4s 6d and the proceeds went to the League of Friends of Ashludie Hospital. The programme included Schumann's 4th symphony, Elgar's *Pomp & Circumstance* and *The Dowie Dens of Yarrow* by Hamish McCunn. John Renwick, the headmaster of Macalpine Primary School, sang Mozart arias and a selection of Scots songs.

The Rodgers and Hammerstein musical *Carousel*, starring Gordon McRae and Shirley Jones, was the film which the J.B. Milne organisation used to open their new 'supercinema', the Capitol, in August 1956. Built on the foundations of what had been Her Majesty's Theatre, latterly the Majestic cinema, the patrons were thrilled by the spacious auditorium which seated 1,400 with a 'Cinemascope' screen 50ft long and 20ft high.

On 1 December 1956 Dick McTaggart fought Harry Kurschat of Germany in the final of the World Lightweight Championship at the Melbourne Olympics. McTaggart's fiery display, the 'snappy counterpunching of the Scottish southpaw' led to a points victory on the vote of all three judges. McTaggart, RAF champion for three years from 1953 to 1955, was the current British lightweight champion. A civic reception was planned for his return by Lord Provost William Hughes.

In March 1958 Mario Lanza sang to an almost full Caird Hall in an ordinary lounge suit. He was not in a good mood because his 'clothes were still on the plane'. His performance gave plenty of evidence of his 'effervescent Latin temperament', being full of overtly theatrical gestures, and his delivery was poorly compared to the other great tenors who had performed in the Caird Hall, John McCormack, Richard Tauber and Gigli. A pianist played Chopin and Debussy during the break but Lanza sang only the 13 items on his programme, eight of which were in Italian, and refused to do any encores. He blew a few kisses and disappeared out a rear door, disappointing the autograph hunters.

If Lanza had had minimal contact with the fans, the next performer might be said to have had too much! On 1 May 1958, teenage idol Tommy Steele played two shows at the Caird Hall before almost 6,000 fans. The event earned huge headlines in the papers the following day: 'Tommy Steele Knocked out. Mobbed on Stage by Teenagers. Stewards Fight to Save Star From Girls. Shirt Ripped Hair Torn Out'. The first house had been trouble-free, except for the noise. The singer had rocked the hall with his half-hour set, which had been broadcast to seven hospitals in the Dundee district, and he evaded the inevitable crush of fans at the end. In the interval he had signed over 30 'Glad Mags' for students to auction for charity and two keen fans, Maureen Hartgetion, a 15-year-old from Montgomerie Square, and 20-year-old Helen Cairney of Mossgiel Crescent, had gifted him an inscribed St Christopher medal in a box. Then he went on stage for the second set. He kicked off with *Rebel Rock* and delighted the organ gallery by turning and playing to them although he had to rebuke two over-vocal fans with a smiling 'Will you please shut up?'

As the excitement built up, the singer was 'almost torn

apart in amazing Caird Hall scenes' at the end of his second show at 10.45pm. Or nearly the end. The singer was midway through *Maybelline* with two chorusses to go when a particularly enthusiastic 'Oh yeah!' was misunderstood by the fans as being the end of the show. Three hundred, mostly girls, pushed over the phalanx of stewards and mobbed the stage. It had been a big mistake to let fans sit in the organ gallery behind the stage because these too leapt to the front with some fans jumping 10ft. The star was surrounded, his way of escape cut off, and he was submerged in a sea of screaming girls. His manager, Larry Parnes, managed to fight his way through but Tommy's right arm had been twisted up his back and his shirt almost ripped off. He shouted 'Let me go!' and screamed in agony as hairs were pulled out of his head. As the battle continued between the fans and the police, the almost unconscious singer, guitar hanging from his neck, was carried by stewards and a *Courier* reporter to the dressing room. The hall door was wedged and ambulance men attended to him and to a girl who had fainted. Then someone switched out all the lights. The chant 'We want Tommy!' went up but the crowd eventually dispersed. One steward opined: 'I thought he was going to be killed.' Half an hour later the singer had recovered and expressed disappointment at not finishing the show. According to his manager, whose watch had been smashed in the fracas, he wanted to go back on and perform. 'I told him the hall had been cleared,' Parnes said, adding, 'he still wants to come back to Dundee.' About 500 fans remained to see the singer carried out by two policemen into his black Rolls-Royce at the Angus Garage at midnight and some followed the car all the way down to Riverside Drive. The visit of Frankie Vaughan later that year was trouble free.

The third of September 1959 was eagerly awaited by 3,000 teenagers as the date when Cliff Richard was to play at the Gaumont. There were to be two shows and tickets were 10s 6d. Predictably there was hysteria at the show and at the Royal Hotel, where the entourage was staying. The support bands were the Kingpins, the Landis Brothers (Britain's answer to the Everlys) and several other bands. Cliff and the Shadows took the stage as the final act and played 10 numbers including *Move It, Never Mind, Mean Streak*, and his million-selling big hit *Livin' Doll*, although little if anything of them could be heard above the screaming. Cliff's every movement in his shiny pink jacket and tie set off waves of hysteria and some girls fainted. The fans tried to prevent Cliff leaving and two girls had to be dragged to safety from under the wheels of a car. Later, Cliff declared he was 'knocked out' by his reception in Dundee. Whether he was being ironic is not known! The

The distinctive Hilltown Clock, erected in 1911, has long been a familiar landmark and in 1957, the public lavatory next to it was still in use. (The Courier, Dundee)

Teenage idol Tommy Steele, brought north on a Larry Parnes' Rock and Roll package tour, was mobbed by fans and knocked unconscious after the second house of his show on 1 May 1958 at the Caird Hall. (The Courier, Dundee)

management of the Royal Hotel was less pleased when in the battle between fans and police a glass swing door was smashed.

In November 1959, the Health Committee passed the clean-air plan to make Dundee a smoke-controlled area in 20 years, after it was estimated that 12.33 tons of grit and ash was falling on each square mile of Dundee every month.

Dundee's first 'self-service' food store opened in December 1959 at 23–25 Victoria Road. W.E. Dryden, fruiterer and florist, hoped the new method would lead to cheaper food. Further down Victoria Road, McGill Brothers, drapers and clothiers, had opened a new building on five floors. Smith Brothers (Dundee) Limited, drapiers, clothiers and outfitters in the nearby Murraygate, were also cashing in, with a score of departments and 250 staff.

Professor James Walker, appointed head of a new midwifery and gynaecology research unit at Dudhope Terrace in May 1958, was awarded a CBE in 1971. His wife Catherine and daughters Joan (left) and Margaret accompanied him to Buckingham Palace. Professor Walker led the fight against deformity and mental defectiveness to ensure Dundonians got 'quality babies'. (The Courier, Dundee)

In the summer up to 20,000 Dundonians made their way to the beaches to participate in events organised by the Broughty Ferry Development Association. The first beach leader, Lindsay Campbell, a final-year engineering student, supervised swimmers, sandcastle building, treasure hunts for buried

objects and 'Beautiful Baby' shows. There were many talent contests, including the Miss Broughty Ferry beauty contest, whose senior and junior winners were chosen at a dance at the Chalet. Bands played on Castle Green and extra buses were put on to cope with the demand.

Beach Crescent, Broughty Ferry, and beach scene, 1957. Sunbathing and swimming at Broughty was a popular pastime at weekends and holidays. (The Courier, Dundee)

Ice skating and ice hockey were popular pursuits at Claypotts as here, on 2 January 1952. In cold weather, the Corporation flooded the park and provided lighting. Complaints from residents over rowdiness finally put an end to the activity in the 1960s. (Evening Telegraph, Dundee)

But the decade ended in tragedy. On 8 December 1959 the brave Broughty lifeboat *Mona* was lost with her eight-man crew in the estuary. At 3.15am she had launched in a full gale to assist the North Carr lightship, which had broken adrift off Fife Ness. At 4.48am, *Mona* radioed that she had cleared the bar and was well. Then silence. At first light, an RAF helicopter took off from Leuchars and the vessel was found stranded on Buddon Sands. Nearby were the bodies of her crew: Ronald Grant, George Watson, George B. Smith, James Ferrier, Alexander Gall, John T. Grieve, John Grieve and David Anderson.

After the Mona *lifeboat disaster on 8 December 1959, when the eight-man crew was lost in a storm, a memorial service was held near Buddon Sands on Christmas Eve, and floral tributes were laid on the now-calmer waters of the Tay Estuary.* (Evening Telegraph, Dundee)

CHAPTER 3

The Space Age Sixties

Reconstruction: A Majestic Mirage?

Kirkton High School had electric under-floor heating and provided meals from the school's own all-electric kitchen, which could produce 750 meals a day. The school also boasted two large gymnasiums, a swimming pool and a 20-acre recreation field. There were 35 classrooms, nine science labs, nine technical rooms, eight domestic science rooms, eight art and craft rooms and three music rooms. To the Corporation, it was 'a palace of Education'. In May 1961, St John's RC Secondary School moved from Park Place to new buildings on a 14-acre site on the northern outskirts. Brother Brice, the headmaster, was

The first pupils admitted to Kirkton High School in February 1960. The school, described as a 'palace of education' was not officially opened until 19 October. It was the largest and most modern in the east of Scotland, serving housing schemes as far apart as Camperdown and Douglas and Angus with a full roll of 1,400. (The Courier, Dundee)

The domestic science class at Kirkton High School, 1960. (The Courier, Dundee)

overjoyed with the new location. 'Here we hear the skylark rising outside the window – very different from being overshadowed by mills and factories.'

Perhaps the most obvious signs of reconstruction were in the city centre. The Courier Building was acquiring a 10-storey tower extension and the tower of

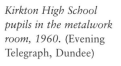

Kirkton High School pupils in the metalwork room, 1960. (Evening Telegraph, Dundee)

Queen's College, nearing completion by the end of 1960, was altering the city's skyline. More than one million pounds of development was planned at Queen's College behind the tower north to Hawkhill and west to Mount Pleasant, and included several new buildings, a new students' union, a male students' residence at Belmont and a dental school with a tower, all based on assumptions that the number of students would ultimately increase to 2,400.

The long-discussed idea of a Tay road bridge was finally going beyond the hot air stage. A traffic census had been conducted in August 1958 and test borings were to be taken to locate the most suitable crossing line. Ex-Lord Provost William Hughes appealed to the public to raise the £10,000 required. The first stage of the inner ring road was underway. By 1963, it seemed as if the heart of the city was in the grip of major surgery. Dundee was well ahead of all other Scottish cities in its extensive, even drastic, renewal programme. The Overgate, where work had barely started, was to be followed by a new Wellgate centre. Dundee, it was said, was the first city attempting to harness private commercial enterprise to municipal planning. The development plan included the replacement of the railway yards, the reclaiming of disused docks and the spur to it all was the road bridge proposal – which forced the solution of traffic problems with an urgency no other city had to contemplate. Much was lost in the demolition to make way for the road bridge landfall. The last ships from the Earl Grey Dock were evicted – private motorboats and sprat yawls moved to the south side of Camperdown Dock, in March 1963 – the 115-year-old Royal Arch was demolished and the rubble was used to fill in the Earl Grey Dock. The inner ring road was to be drawn tightly around the central area, at a distance of less than two miles, creating the urgent need to review parking space. Two years later, a new one-way system was inaugurated in east central Dundee, with parking restrictions introduced in the Seagate, Wellgate and St Andrews Street. In some central streets there was to be no waiting at anytime. The crowning jewel of the plan was a municipal airport – Dundee, it was proposed, would be the only city to have an airport within a mile of its city centre.

The Corporation approved the phased redevelopment of the Overgate and in January 1961 the bulldozers moved in. Among the premises which disappeared were Wilsons Bonanza Stores; Meltoy; Thomas Machir hairdressers; George Heinan, fishmonger; Christies the drapers; A.W. Watson motor hirers; the 60 Minute Cleaners; Alex Marshall the ladies' hairdresser; and the Dundee Eastern Co-operative Society. The digging disturbed hundreds of jumbled skeletons and skulls in the mass graves left after General Monk's seige of 1651.

The Washington Café in Nethergate on the front of the 'old' Overgate had been a popular meeting place since the war. It was one of the casualties when the bulldozers moved in to clear the ground for the 'new' Overgate in January 1961. The owner, Steve Barbieri, gave up after 50 years in business. (Evening Telegraph, Dundee)

The last train to run from Dundee West Station leaves for Glasgow, May 1965. (The Courier, Dundee)

While many applauded the headlong rush to redevelop, others bemoaned the loss of some fine buildings. Many deplored the new concrete brutalism of the city centre. Julie Davidson, writing in the *Scotsman*, described the new city as 'a majestic mirage… so disenchanting at close quarters. Only a native could find beauty in Dundee,' she claimed. 'Disparaging assessments,' she added, 'are no longer disputed. Part of the armoury against them is the existence of a plan to overcome the city's aesthetic shortcomings'. To Dundonians the plan mainly seemed to consist of knocking things down and putting up uglier buildings. For example the new Littlewoods store, opened by Lord Provost Alex MacKenzie in October 1968, was, with some 16,000sq ft including a 2,000sq ft cafeteria and 160 staff, a useful new retail outlet, but by no stretch of the imagination could it be considered visually appealing.

As work on the road bridge continued, it was claimed that it was already a tourist attraction. Engineers were coming to view the work in progress but tragedy struck, firstly on 11 November 1965, when, at 10pm, a 90-foot section of the temporary bridge structure suddenly collapsed, toppling a crane, two bogies, a hut and three men into the river. Two empty lifejackets were recovered but 25-year-olds John McQueen of Ballindean Road and Donald Ross of Pennycook Lane, and 50-year-old James Lennie of Abernethy, had drowned. Just 10 weeks later, the managing director of the contractors, 52-year-old William Logan, died when his small plane crashed near Inverness on 22 January 1966. He was described as 'a legend... with integrity, determination and the gift of natural leadership.'

But with the mighty bridge nearing completion, anxiety about traffic congestion became acute. Where, it was demanded, would the 6,000 vehicles per day from the Tay road bridge park? Would there be congestion at Blackscroft, or in Nethergate? These fears were not realised, for in the first year of its operation, 2.3 million vehicles crossed the Tay road bridge, and two years later the figures had passed the 3 million mark, without severe disruption in the city. Soon, it seemed as if the bridge had always been there. At first there were occasional breakdowns on the bridge, often due to lack of petrol. These would cost a driver a 30s penalty, or 50s if it was found to be due to an empty petrol tank. There was, however, only one serious accident, when a van

Demolition work creeps nearer to the West Station in September 1965. (The Courier, Dundee)

Dundee's spectacular West Station, despite appeals from many quarters for its preservation, is finally demolished in May 1966. (The Courier, Dundee)

The Queen Mother opened the £4 million Tay Road Bridge on Thursday 18 August 1966. 70,000 took advantage of a three-day toll-free offer and drove across the bridge on the first weekend. (The Courier, Dundee)

toppled against the central reservation in high winds. The highest daily cross rate was 10,000.

In 1965, the Town Planning department released a detailed plan of expected population growth over the next two decades. It anticipated a population rise from 182,959 to 198,400 in that period. The areas expected to expand most were the Claverhouse, Fintry, Mid Craigie, Douglas and Angus areas, with more modest rises in Ancrum Road, Camperdown, Lochee and Menzieshill. St Mary's and Kirkton would increase from 23,291 to 32,500. West Ferry and Broughty Ferry would increase by 50 percent in each case. Almost no change was expected in the Lawside, Hilltown, Clepington Road and Craigiebank areas but some areas were expected to decline, particularly the West End (from 17,993 to 9,200).

The Angus Hotel, a distinctive if banal monolith, was a cornerstone of the 'new' Overgate development in 1964. (The Courier, Dundee)

Out on the western periphery at the 231-acre site at Ninewells, the teaching hospital and medical school were taking shape, a joint venture between the Eastern Regional Hospital Board and St Andrews University. Work started in summer 1964 with a labour force peaking at 700. The Hospital Board anticipated employing 2,000 staff. The hospital would have 31 wards, with 761 patient beds, and a car park capable of holding 900 cars.

In November 1964, Kingsway Technical College was opened by Scottish Secretary William Ross. It had incorporated the old Dundee Trades School and already needed a new annexe because of the pressure of numbers; 1,992 part-time day and 2,048 part-time evening students. The College of Commerce opened its new seven-storey Constitution Road building in 1969. Planning had begun 10 years earlier for a site in Park Place, then construction started in Barrack Road in July 1966.

Whitfield Primary School opened in October 1968,

The old and the new. Slum areas in North William Street and the Alexander Street multis being constructed in 1967. (The Courier, Dundee)

on the edge of the countryside, with a 'twin', St Matthew's RC Primary, being constructed less than 100 yards away. All children initially attended Whitfield. The headmaster, Hamish MacKenzie, was very pleased with the open-air feeling inside the school, its under-floor heating, the school's low, square, imposing profile, and the unobtrusive wire perimeter fence. More attention was at last being paid to the peripheral areas. The Lea Rig pub opened in Douglas and Angus with gas-fired central heating, lounge bar, public bar and cocktail bar. It was as if someone had finally looked beyond the mirage to see where the ordinary people lived.

Housing Allocation and the Owner-Occupier Sector

In 1960, there were eight firms building homes for sale in Dundee. The preference was for bungalows, though there was a gradually increasing demand for more rooms, with the three or four apartment homes being superseded by houses with three or four bedrooms. Semi-detached chalet bungalows with two upstairs bedrooms might feature a 'dinette' in place of a separate dining room. Building was booming in Balgillo Road, Claypotts and at Invergowrie. Most builders agreed that only purchasers of the more expensive houses would express interest in central heating 'and even then the idea takes a bit of selling', according to one estate agent, who considered that less than 2 percent of Dundee clients looked on it as an essential or even desirable feature. Some of the new houses had their own garages, which might add between £175 and £200 to the price.

There was much interest in the Betts showhouse at Gillies Terrace, featuring the Bett Lomond design, in April 1960. 'One of the most attractive I have seen,' was a comment included in an advertising feature at the time. The asking price for the three-bedroom house was £2,895. The Angus Construction company began building a private 150-house estate at Claverhouse, which was to be landscaped and surrounded by parkland. More than 400 houses were built in a year by private builders but land was already becoming scarcer within the city boundaries.

In 1967 Dundee had 66,129 houses, of which only about 25 percent were owner-occupied, considerably less than any other Scottish city or the average figure of 55 percent in English cities. Partly, this could be explained by Selective Employment Tax and other factors which had increased the price of houses. In 1967 a three-apartment house sold for £3,300, compared with £1,900 for the same house in 1958–9. The main reason for low rates of owner-occupation was probably the enthusiasm with which the council provided housing at relatively low rent. Even families with a reasonably high income did not apparently feel the need to buy a new house. Around 1,000 second-hand properties sold in the Dundee area in a year. Overall, the highest rate of housing turnover was in West Ferry and Broughty Ferry, which were also the areas of most recent development. The West End remained popular but did not have the same turnover. Houses were on average £300 cheaper in Dundee in 1967 than in Glasgow and £500 cheaper than in Edinburgh or Aberdeen.

For those – the vast majority – who looked to the Corporation for their housing needs, there were strict rules of allocation. The highest priority was given to those who were badly housed, either by being in overcrowded areas, or in areas of slum clearance. Except in cases of outright medical priority referred by a Medical Officer of Health, or a family made homeless by tempest, flood or fire, an applicant would not qualify until they had been in continuous provable residence in the city for at least five years and their application had been on the waiting list for at least one year. An extra qualification was required from newly-married couples. They would not be considered until they had been married for at least one year. With approximately 13,000 on the housing list, applications were dealt with on the basis of their date, but the applicant's preferences had an important bearing on their prospects.

The Corporation was producing ever-greater numbers of houses at a cheaper unit cost. Per head of the population, Dundee's output was greater than any other city in Britain, and by 1966, 86 percent of all dwellings constructed since the war were council houses. One method was multi-storey housing. Opened on a wintry day in January 1960, the two multi-blocks in Dryburgh offered two and three-room flats at a rent of £1 13s 7d per week for a three room flat, which included rates of 16s 6d. Two-room flats cost £1 8s 3d.

In July 1965, 678 prefabs were still in use in the city, in Macalpine Road, Barnhill, Glamis Road, Craigie Drive, Kingsway East, Elgin Street, Graham Street and here in Blackshade. (Evening Telegraph, Dundee)

The two Dryburgh multi-storey blocks opened in January 1960, with two-room and three-room flats, at a weekly rent of £1 13s 7d and £1 8s 3d, which included rates of 16s 6d. (Evening Telegraph, Dundee)

A year and a half later, more multis opened at Dryburgh and Foggyley. Most of the new tenants had been transferred from old tenements with shared toilets and outside stairs. All had been taken from the general waiting list in strict order of their application, irrespective of family size and whether there were young children. Quite soon after the first tenants moved in fears began to be raised about the chest-high verandas outside the kitchen doors. The wrought iron verandahs – no doubt a gleam in the architect's eye – looked remarkably like climbing frames. Building work continued at Menzieshill from 1963–5 and included five 15-storey blocks. Ardler, in 1964–7, included a network of patio houses and the cottage type with six monstrous 17-storey blocks in the centre, which dominated the city skyline. Each had 298 dwellings.

In July 1965, work began on more tall buildings – skyscrapers – at Dallfield. It was the 'dawning of a new era,' according to Housing Convenor Tom Moore. 'A previously congested area is being transformed into a traffic free spacious and modern development worthy of one of the most commanding sites in the city'. The four blocks with 84 houses in each cost the Corporation £1.5 million. This meant that the apartments were costing £4,000 each, but this was put down to the extra expense of building vertically. New high-rise housing was planned for Maxwelltown and Old Glamis Road.

Housing unit costs became even cheaper when Crudens of Musselburgh built the Bison factory at Trottick in April 1967 to produce components for industrialised building. Much of the distinctive deck-access housing at Whitfield was constructed of prefab units from the Crudens factory in Dundee. In 1968, 620 units were available, with 80 produced each month after that, and the first 2,500 were for Whitfield. The factory built tubing for electrics into concrete, and window units were delivered ready glazed. The 15-storey multi – Trottick Court – was completed in nine months, by 21 June 1968. But statistics revealed that although slum areas were being demolished at a rate of over 400 houses each year, almost half (48.5 percent) of the city's houses in 1966 had no bath, with 24.9 percent forced to share an outside toilet. On the other hand, Dundee Corporation was among the first to convert houses to all-electric in 1959, and by March 1963, a total of 18,002 had been completed. Local authority delegations came from far and near to inspect them.

Peter Doig was Labour's candidate for the Dundee West by-election in November 1963. At this election meeting in the Rialto cinema, Lochee, he is supported by Lord Provost McManus and George Brown MP, leader of the Labour opposition. (Evening Telegraph, Dundee)

Dundee's Industrial Boom

In June 1960 Maurice McManus, the newly elected Lord Provost, opened the Dundee Readymix Concrete plant at Longtown Street. It was the fourth such plant in Scotland, the only one north of the Forth, and provided a huge impetus to building and civil engineering contracts in the area, since normally concreting would have to be discontinued in frosty weather but could now take place all year round, with fewer seasonal lay-offs.

> Maurice McManus was a former Midlothian miner who settled in Dundee – 'this beautiful city' as he often called it – and worked for the Hydro-Board. He spent 28 years in local politics and represented the Kirkton-Downfield area, latterly as a Tayside regional councillor, before retiring in 1981. His seven years as Provost (1960–7) might have been extended had he not lost on a cut of the cards to Alexander Mackenzie in 1967. He was a prime mover on some of the most important modernisation projects of the 1950s and 1960s, including: making Queen's College a separate university; the Tay road bridge; new schools; the founding the Citizen of the Year Award; and attracting industry. Known as 'Mr Industry' for his commitment to the area, he received an honorary doctorate from Dundee University and in 1964 the CBE. In July 1982, four months after receiving the freedom of the city, he died aged 75.

Dundee's industrial development was continuing strongly and attracting praise from the Board of Trade. The Conservative Secretary of State had referred in the House of Commons to the city's expansion since 1945 with 105 approved projects, a total of 3 million sq ft of factory space and nearly 13,000 additional jobs. At the end of 1964 the Dundee unemployment rate at 2.2 percent was the lowest for six years and below the Scottish average of 3.4 percent, although above the UK average of 1.5 percent. (see *Appendix, Figure 4*)

Dundee's 'Mr Industry' Lord Provost Maurice McManus. (Evening Telegraph, Dundee)

A busy harbour scene with jute liners Purnea *and* Aziz Bhatti *at the Queen Elizabeth Wharf,* Mamoor *at King George Wharf,* Lyminge *at Caledon West Wharf and* Safina-e-Ismail *at Eastern Wharf, 4 February 1967.* (Evening Telegraph, Dundee)

The popular 'Fifie' Scotscraig had been in service as a car ferry since May 1942 but was sold soon after the road bridge opened, and with its 'sister' Abercraig was towed to Southampton in February 1968. There had been vessels of that name on the Tay since 1812. Both subsequently ended up as tourist pleasure craft in Malta. (Evening Telegraph, Dundee)

By 1962 the Caledon yard was in a battle for survival. The capacity of British shipyards was double the annual rate of orders. Caledon invested £250,000 in new machinery that year, having already spent £1 million since the war. The main welding shed was doubled in size and another pair of 15-ton cranes was installed. A new Messer burning machine was introduced. This electronically controlled the cutting of steel plate to the exact size from one-tenth size drawings fed into it. Caledon also ordered a new Goliath travelling crane. The yard was determined to remain at the forefront of shipbuilding.

The 20 years of the Dundee industrial estates had seen the creation of 2 million sq ft of factory space, with 17 tenants employing 10,000 on the three industrial estates and two individual sites in Dundee. There was substantial expansion at NCR, Timex and Ferranti. The NCR factory built at Camperdown in 1945 had actually preceded the industrial estate, which was less than half a mile away. In 1967 they had, apart from Camperdown, six other factories, occupying nearly two-thirds of the total floor space (820,000sq ft out of 1,356,811) of the industrial estate, with 4,200 employees. By July 1969, NCR orders exceeded 1,700 with turnover set to top £20 million. The Gourdie factory turned out Century 100 computers for customers in France, Germany and the Netherlands, and Dundee engineers were sent for training to the NCR electronics plant at Hawthorne, California, to learn about testing and installing the Century 200 series. NCR's comprehensive decimalisation programme was in top gear: 140,000 sets of components for conversion of accounting machines and cash registers were manufactured. Dual-currency machines and photo micro-image readers designed by Dundee engineers would continue to attract large orders.

Timex employed 3,400, a 40 percent increase over 18 months due to the manufacture of the instant-developing Polaroid camera and increasing production of watches. It was the largest supplier of British-made watches to the home market. Veeder Root opened a new factory at Gourdie, taking on an extra 125 employees to construct counting and computing devices, vending machines, coin-op machines, and an electric predeterminator unit.

Switch On The Sixties

In January 1960 Scott Fyfe (Motors) Ltd opened the first modern petrol service station at Seagate, the company also being the first to introduce girls as forecourt attendants in their East Kingsway garage. In September 1960, after an absence of three years, Dundee's Own exhibition was back at the Caird Hall with the emphasis firmly on entertainment and gadgets for the consumer. There was a popular display of closed-circuit TV, where visitors could see themselves on a TV screen, and a mouse circus in the upper gallery, with mice working all sorts of wierd gadgets. Model cars raced around a spectacular race track. The RAF display included a model sputnik to take you on a trip to the moon for 6d, complete with flashing red lights and flickering indicator panel.

*The British Eagle
advance party unloading
signs for the Dundee Air
Terminal. Mr R.E.
Smith, traffic manager at
Glasgow, with two
station assistants, Mr D.
McEachern (left) and Mr
Ian McNeil. In July
1966, a 36-seater British
Eagle Dove DC 3 made
the inaugural flight to
Glasgow.* (The Courier,
Dundee)

*The Wellgate Steps in
October 1961.* (The
Courier, Dundee)

*Next page: Looking
down the Wellgate,
September 1965.*
(Evening Telegraph,
Dundee)

Housewives thrilled to the new Singer Slant-o-matic, billed as 'the greatest step forward in sewing since the machine was invented'. There was a wide range of TVs on display in the Marryat Hall, and for the first time, a brand new Colston dishwasher. The 1960s revolution in technology was having an impact on Dundee consumers. By 30 September 1960 there were 44,310 TV licence holders in Dundee compared to only 38,175 in 1959.

In August 1961, BBC Radio conducted a Dundee experiment, producing a programme of local news, interviews and gramophone record requests from Dundee, based at Coldside Library. The station went 'live', although only on VHF, at 6.35am on 24 August 1961: 'This is Radio Dundee…' Not everyone was happy about the idea and several expressed anxiety about uncouth language or 'the inarticulate lack of polite expression' of ordinary interviewees. What might slip out, they asked, 'in unguarded moments?'

In summer 1964, a new TV mast was erected on the Law. BBC viewers were instructed that they might have to adjust their aerials. Grampian TV went on air for the first time on 13 October 1965. The saltire logo appeared on screen at 6pm, followed at 6.06pm by a short welcome to viewers and *The Wednesday People*, a weekly magazine programme. In July 1967, BBC 2 broadcast in colour for the first time. Electricity was the key to a brighter future and in

G.L. Wilson's department store, 'The Corner' and the Murraygate in September 1961.
(Evening Telegraph, Dundee)

1964 thousands flocked to the Hydro-Electric Board's Go-Electric '64 exhibition in the Caird Hall. Four years later the Hydro-Electric Board announced that the number of Dundee consumers had doubled in 25 years, from 36,700 consumers in 1943, and the city's power consumption had risen from 20 megawatts in 1943 to 218 megawatts. Dundonians were switching on the sixties.

The Invention of Teenagers

In March 1960, the Modern Miss department at Andrew Birrell and Sons shoe shop announced that only one of their nine assistants was over 20 because 'the modern young woman from 15 to 20 prefers to be served by someone of her own age'. In the world of teenage fashion, the Modern Miss had never had it so good. While many men still flocked to Burtons, Alexander Caird and Sons Ltd had been expanding rapidly after the war in their Reform Street department store and hoped to keep up their high standards of quality. They made suits and kilts to measure but were finding that off-the-peg clothes made of synthetic fibres in more adventurous styles were far more popular. In 1962, the local paper reported 'Teenager opens new hair salon'. This was Aileen in Nethergate, named after the 19-year-old daughter of George Ross, the owner of a ladies' hairdressers in King Street. One of the most popular new hairdos was 'the Twist'.

Bingo – or, as it was first known, housey-housey – came to Dundee in August 1961 when two venues opened in cinemas. The Rialto Bingo & Social Club in Lochee held Saturday night sessions. Admission cost 2s, the same price as a session of five cards. The Royal Bingo Club in Arthurstone Terrace offered Monday and Wednesday evening sessions. 'We've got 600 members already,' the owners declared. 'We offer a guaranteed jackpot of £20 although it could be considerably more.' On its opening day, a queue of 400 waited from midday to 1.15pm outside the Rialto for the opening session, although both clubs were quick to point out that bingo would not detract from the main operation of the cinemas. They weren't sure whether bingo would 'catch on'. The Revd John Beaumont of Fairmuir Church, Moderator of the Church of Scotland, was saddened by the arrival of bingo. 'As far as I know the effect has not been good when it has been introduced elsewhere,' he said. 'I'm sorry it's started in Dundee.'

In October 1962, *Dr No*, the first Bond film, enthralled audiences in Dundee and Fred Iannetta opened an ice cream factory in Maitland Street capable of producing 100 gallons of fresh ice cream each hour. His shop in the Hawkhill was a favourite for a Saturday night 'McCallum' – ice cream with raspberry on it. With 10 vans he operated a daily service to each housing scheme in Dundee.

Twist marathons were all the rage. Over four days 20,000 packed the JM Ballroom to watch the 40-odd competitors gyrating and shuffling. Several competitors lost their jobs because they took part rather than go to work.

A polio outbreak in
Fintry in June 1962 led
to the dispensing of
sugar cubes containing
anti-polio vaccine at
Fintry welfare clinic.
(Evening Telegraph,
Dundee)

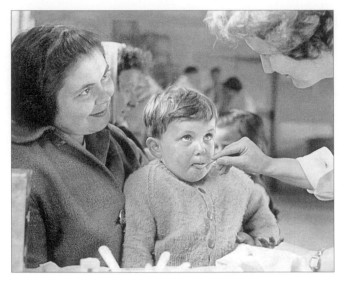

A polio outbreak in Fintry in June 1962 led to the dispensing of sugar cubes containing anti-polio vaccine at Fintry welfare clinic. (Evening Telegraph, Dundee)

Left: Marathon twist king Bobby Cannon with a pacer. The 19-year-old trainee hotel manager from Pitlochry gyrated nonstop for 94 hours 50 minutes in the JM Ballroom in March 1962 to collect top prize of £10 plus £1 for every hour he danced, a total of £105. (Evening Telegraph, Dundee)

Right: Mrs Cathy Connelly of Craighill Place, holder of the world title in twisting marathons relaxes with her daughter Elaine and son James after a hard day's twisting. (The Courier, Dundee)

Friends of Bobby Cannon had hired a bus to cheer him on. Dundee was later famous for its twist experts: Fritz Wilson, Derek Kidd, Lindsay 'Rubber Legs' Bogan and Mrs Cathy Connelly. For many, the Haparanda coffee bar in Arbroath Road was an important part of their social life. Ciano Soave, the owner, took a personal interest in his patrons. He was described as having a 'friendly big brother manner', which meant that he was confided in and there was rarely trouble at the 'Hap.'

Trouble was on the minds of the Caird Hall staff when they heard of the forthcoming concert by American rockers Gene Vincent and Eddie Cochrane on 23 February 1960. Taking advice from promoter Larry Parnes, no tickets had been sold for the organ gallery section behind the stage. But things started badly as soon as the lights went down when the audience, mainly girls with an average age of 15, began screaming. The lights were switched on again in an effort to curb the 'bad behaviour' but the audience sat up on the backs of their

seats and crowded to the front, where a wall of hefty stewards – mainly ex-wrestlers – lined the stagefront. When Gene Vincent, in a black leather jacket, appeared on the stage a general brawl broke out, started (according to the police) by members of a gang barred from the local dance halls. The City Factor was hauled unceremoniously off the stage by his ankles, a large screen was sent flying by a mass of fighting bodies and the bronze bust of Sir James Caird was toppled from its stand. Vincent did nothing to discourage the riot. It took more than 12 uniformed policemen to restore order. Later, backstage, Vincent resented the way one local musician was looking at him. 'What the **** are you lookin' at?' he snarled, pulling out a flick-knife.

Things were much calmer, if not quieter, on 7 October 1963 when the Beatles played the Caird Hall as the final stopping-off point in a weekend tour of three one-night performances. It was the second time the band had played in Scotland, having previously toured small dance halls in the north as the Silver Beatles. The bill included Malcolm Clark and the Crestas, who opened the show with *Memphis Tennessee* and *Some Other Guy Now* (a Lennon-

Ciano Soave with patrons of his popular Haparanda coffee bar in Arbroath Road in November 1970. The 'Hap' operated from 1958 to 1972 and the Saturday night dances were generally trouble-free. Ciano was educated at St John's High School and then worked in his father's fish and chip shop in Baffin Street. He was awarded the CBE for his services to young people in 1965 and died in August 1999, aged 73. (The Courier, Dundee)

Frenzied scenes at the Gene Vincent concert in the Caird Hall, 23 February 1960. (The Courier, Dundee)

Frenzied scenes at the Gene Vincent concert in the Caird Hall, 23 February 1960. (The Courier, Dundee)

McCartney song). Next up were a local band, Johnny Hudson and the Teen-Beats. Hudson, whose real name was Johnny Moran, was soon to join the Hamburg-bound Dundee band the Hi Four. A girl duo, the Caravelles, were next, singing *Abilene* and *You Don't Have To Be a Baby To Cry*. The

In July 1963 the educational cruise ship Devonia, *with 1,026 school pupils on board, left Dundee for a two-week cruise around the Baltic, calling in at Oslo, Leningrad, Helsinki and Copenhagen. For most, this was their first trip abroad.* (Evening Telegraph, Dundee)

The Beatles in the Caird Hall having a 'cuppa' before their show, 20 October 1964. (The Courier, Dundee)

Overlanders were a folk group whose set included *If I Had A Hammer*. The two shows were back to back over four hours and the Beatles first appeared onstage in the dimmed lights at 7.40pm to face thousands of 'bobbing weaving, shrieking devotees… the Mersey moppets, high priests of the most compulsive and commercial sound… frantic shouted vocals with falsetto top notes…' The *Courier* reporter felt that his ears were 'bludgeoned by the noise'.

Lennon missed half of the first number because his amp cable was hopelessly entangled but the band gamely played without him. The band played nine numbers in their 25-minute spot, including *From Me To You, I'll Get You, Taste of Honey, Saw Her Standing There, Baby It's You* and their hit single *She Loves You*, before ending with *Twist and Shout*. Little of this could be heard because of the incessant screaming and even a good-natured 'Shut up!' from Lennon only brought a greater answering howl. The critic enjoyed the event, penning

a large review 'Beatles, You're The Tops!' The band and the rest of the tour stayed overnight in the Salutation Hotel, Perth.

One year later, it was 'A Mad, Glad Night With The Beatles' as the band played their second concert in the Caird Hall on 20 October 1964. 'Beatles on the wane?' asked the local reporter, 'absolute rubbish!' Some 6,000 fans stood outside the hall screaming and shouting 'We love you Beatles!' Scores of ambulance men and Red Cross workers were kept busy with fainting girls – a total of 50 casualties on the night. The other bands on the bill included Brian Epstein's new 'discoveries' Michael Haslam and the Rustiks, the Remo Four and Tommy Quickly, who provided the final warm-up, while Mary Wells, a glamorous black singer, turned in a perfomance 'more suited to a London night spot'. Strangely the audience maintained complete silence for Sounds Incorporated's instrumental versions of *Maria* and the *William Tell Overture* – and politely applauded at the end. This was the versatile band which had backed Gene Vincent!

By the time the Beatles came on they were faced with 'ear-splitting bedlam'. They grinned, waved and tried to be heard as jellybabies rained down on them from the balconies. Forty powerful stewards repulsed the fans while another 35 'Beatle-protecting giants' patrolled the aisles. The band ended with *Long Tall Sally* and it was all over.

On 18 June 1965 it was the turn of the Rolling Stones. Their first house had sold only 800 tickets and the second a more respectable 1,400. What the fans lacked in numbers, they made up for in enthusiasm. Forty girls had to be carried out. One made it onto the stage and threw her arms around Mick Jagger. The officials regarded it as the 'worst since the Tommy Steele riots'. The Stones were supported by the Hollies, an American singer called Doris Troy who sang three songs before she had to go off with sinus trouble, Mike and the Shades, the West Five and the Modells. The Stones made a very smooth getaway via side doors and Castle Street to a limousine and stayed at the Gleneagles Hotel during their four-day tour of Scotland.

Another famous visitor, on 14 February 1966, was 'the lad 'imself,' comic Tony Hancock, who did a 35-minute spot at the Theatre Royal in Castle Street. Prior to the show he was asked by a member of staff at the blood transfusion unit at DRI to give blood and he did so during the afternoon. It was claimed this was his first and only time as a blood donor and that this Dundee experience must be the genesis of the famous 'blood donor' sketch, although the sketch was well established before the Dundee show. The blood transfusion staff turned out at his show to thank him for his useful publicity.

The Caird Hall 'swung' on 16 February 1967 to Duke Ellington and his band, who drew a large crowd of 2,300 – nearly capacity – at the Caird Hall with a top ticket price of 25 shillings. 'The audience,' reported the *Courier*, 'loved the Duke. He thought they were "beautiful" and told them so.'

The Queen was in Dundee on 30 May 1969. She received a warm welcome on her first visit for 14 years, wearing a vivid yellow outfit on a warm sunny

The Queen Mother arrives at the Caird Hall for the ceremonial granting of full independent status to Dundee University on 1 August 1967. (The Courier, Dundee)

The Queen chats to
workers at the
Douglasfield jute works,
May 1967. (The
Courier, Dundee)

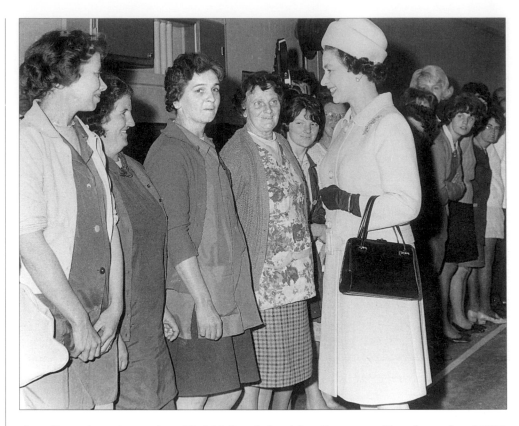

day. Crowds estimated at 50,000 lined the 13-mile route. She chatted to NCR workers at Gourdie and visited Dudhope Court, Lochee, where she received a bouquet from 10-year-old Lynn Kelly, a pupil of the nearby School for the Deaf. The royal entourage went up by lift to the eighth floor for a panoramic view, before returning to City Square for lunch in City Chambers, watched by thousands, including two girls perched on the roof of the partially reconstructed Boots building. The crowd watched as, instead of the Queen coming down the red carpet, a young chef in brilliant whites hurried across the square, vaulted a crush barrier and returned moments later carrying a beautiful cream gateaux in each hand. To the cheers of the crowd he juggled both with one hand and swept off his tall hat with a deep bow, a true performer.

The Sporting Sixties

At Tannadice, Dundee United were taking giant strides after the appointment of Jerry Kerr. His 12 years as manager were to be a momentous period in the club's history. Kerr built up the squad around the giant centre-half Ron Yeats who was soon to transfer to Liverpool. The establishing of Dundee United Sportsman's Clubs and Taypools resulted in increased funding to buy new players and led within four years to promotion to the First Division. After a close rivalry with Hamilton for the League flag, the decider was the home game against Berwick Rangers on 30 April 1960. The 16,000-strong crowd

cheered on their team in the distinctive white strips with two black hoops and Tommy Campbell scored on the two-minute mark. With no further scoring, United were in the First Division. Dundee United became a full-time club and began the new season strongly. After three games they were top of the table

Ecstatic crowds in City Square welcome home the League champions. (Evening Telegraph, Dundee)

and – what was better – they had beaten their rivals, Dundee, 3-1 in front of a 20,000 crowd at Tannadice in August 1960.

The Dark Blues had their first taste of European football in September when they beat IFC Cologne. They defeated Sporting Lisbon 4-1 at Dens on 31 October 1962, beat Anderlecht and finally faced AC Milan in the semi-final, losing on aggregate 5-2 having won the second leg at Dens on 1 May 1963 1-0. A year later, on 25 April 1964, Dundee FC made it to the Scottish Cup final, losing to Rangers 3-1 at Hampden having conceded two very late goals.

The Rise of Teenage Crime

In the mid-1960s the gang problem in Dundee's peripheral areas was attracting a lot of attention. There were dozens of gangs. Fintry, Douglas and Angus, Menzieshill, Kirkton and Charleston were all suffering. The local paper filled pages with interviews and focussed on each scheme to try to find explanations and solutions to the problem. In April 1967, Chief Constable John H. Orr

stated that the juvenile delinquency rate had never been higher. He blamed affluence. 'Youngsters now expect the good things in life as their right. If they can't earn them, they steal them. This is especially true where clothes are concerned… to be up with fashion, many of them will not hesitate to break into the shop which has the type of "gear" they prefer.' Recently, he claimed, two youths had climbed onto the roof of a shop in the centre of town, smashed in through a window and dropped into the premises. They had then carefully selected two black leather jackets, two suede jackets, two shortie overcoats, two pairs of trousers, five sweaters, three cravats, 15 pairs of cufflinks and three pairs of Chelsea boots. It seemed likely that the suspects were 'Mods'.

There was a big upsurge in crimes of violence. The Kirkton Huns conducted a lengthy vendetta against a fish and chip shopkeeper. The Douglas Mafia spat on an elderly man on a bus. Two hundred teenagers armed with shovels and sticks rampaged the streets, turning over a car; hordes of girls ran into the sea fully clothed and rolled in the sand to show off. Gangs buzzed around on scooters, motorcycles and even in cars – and were chased by policemen on

Dundee FC team picture, 20 April 1962, eight days before that crucial match at Muirton, including many of Bob Shankly's famous squad. Front row: (left to right) P. Liney, R. Wishart, A. Gilzean, R. Waddle, R. Seith, G. Smith. Back row: A. Penman, I. Ure, R. Cox, A. Hamilton, A. Cousin, H. Robertson. (Evening Telegraph, Dundee)

Lord Provost McManus with Dundee FC players and officials before the celebratory dinner in the City Chambers, which in honour of the occasion was decorated with blue and white floral displays, 24 August 1962. (The Courier, Dundee)

bicycles. On apprehending a youth, a constable was forced to leave his bicycle and walk to the nearest police box. The police response was to increase the number of plain-clothes officers and to supply officers with personal pocket radios. The Regional Crime Squad might be called in at the invitation of the chief constable, but there was a general perception that the Tay and Forth bridges had aided the rise of crime by affording criminals an easy getaway.

In 1967 the police began a murder hunt when a five-year-old girl's body was discovered in a wardrobe in Kincardine Street, in the 'Blue Mountains' off Hawkhill, in a flea-infested flat. Later that year, one of the city's most notorious crimes hit national headlines. On 1 November 1967, a slight, sandy-haired young man dressed in the uniform of a private in the Gordon Highlanders burst into a top-storey classroom at St John's RC Secondary School in Harefield Road, where 11 Form 3 girls in their early teens were doing needlework with their teacher, Mrs Nanette Hanson. The youth, 19-year-old Robert Francis Mone, was AWOL from his unit. It was the first lesson of the afternoon. Mone took a double-barrelled shotgun from behind his back and shouted at the girls to line up against the wall. He took out ammunition. 'Get back against that wall,' he shouted. 'I've enough ammunition here to blow every one of your heads off and I'll do it if I have to!' Mone ordered the teacher and girls into a dark storeroom. Some were hysterical and in the pandemonium, Mone went around asking their ages in a loud voice, staring directly at them. He said he had been expelled from the school and had come to get his own back on one of the staff. 'Mrs Hanson was marvellous,' one of the girls later testified. 'She kept very calm.'

Mone took six girls out of the room and made them blockade the door with desks. A teacher from the adjacent classroom heard the noise and knocked on the door. Mone fired through the glass panel. He took three girls out one at a time and when they returned they were speechless with sheer terror. His behaviour became increasingly bizarre. He asked Mrs Hanson her age, took off her spectacles and stamped on them. He sneered that she was a pensioner. By this time the police had arrived and surrounded the school. He was urged to give himself up. He declared that he would only let the girls go if an acquaintance of his, Marion Young, was brought in. The police agreed. He then put down the gun and began washing his hair, then started singing. Marion Young was brought in. He let the girls go. 'Not you,' he said to Mrs Hanson. 'You're not going. I want you here.' She was later shot in the back and died. 'Nobody could have been braver than she was. I shall never forget her,' said one of the girls. 'She couldn't have done more for us.' At the end of a two-hour seige, Mone was arrested and remanded in custody. He was judged to be an incurable psychopath and ordered to be detained for life at Carstairs secure mental institution.

An ambulance rushes 26-year-old teacher Mrs Nanette Hanson from St John's Secondary School to hospital moments after the two-hour seige ended on 1 November 1967. Robert Mone had shot her in the back. 'Nobody could have been braver than she was', said one of the terrorised schoolgirls. Mrs Hanson was awarded a posthumous Albert Medal. (The Courier, Dundee)

CHAPTER 4

Construction and Diversity

The Melancholy Monoliths

In 1971, developers Ravenseft and Murrayfield claimed that the £4 million Overgate had completely transformed the centre of Dundee and become, like the Tay Bridge, a tourist attraction in its own right. 'It was,' they claimed, 'our most successful scheme in Scotland.' Out of a total of 143 units only 18 were unoccupied when the final phase, containing an eight-storey office block, 36 shops, two stores, a police station and public conveniences, was completed. The Overgate was the first town centre redevelopment in Scotland and the first where private developers operated under a long lease from the local authority. It significantly boosted the retail sector to 2,000 shops, of which half were in the city centre.

A view of the mid-section of the 'new' Overgate in June 1970. (Evening Telegraph, Dundee)

But there was another side to the coin. The 'old' Overgate had been a thriving warren of small streets, a busy social centre with some housing. When the shops closed in the evening the 'new' Overgate became a gloomy deserted landscape, a muggers' paradise with plenty of shadowy corners and escape routes. The *Scotsman* journalist Julie Davidson noted the 'melancholy nature of the city centre after 6pm.' The city had been brutalised by 'clumsy, ruthless change.' Dundee, she concluded, had become a 'sad city of monolithic filing cabinets'. The American writer Paul Theroux who visited nine years later described it in *Kingdom By The Sea* as 'an interesting monstrosity… a prison-like city of stony-faced order that I associate with the future.'

But the authorities pushed on with wholesale modernisation. In May 1972, it was announced that 23 areas of the city were to be 'given a facelift'. This meant further demolitions, albeit on a smaller scale. There was development on the riverfront which became the 'beige cuboid' Earl Grey Hotel for the Stakis chain. In front of it (but not managing to hide it) was a casino block. Next to it was the leisure centre, completed in 1974 and described by Paul Theroux as having 'the look of a Russian interrogation headquarters, a vast drab Lubyanka in rain-soaked concrete'. The popular Shore Terrace bus depot was cleared to make way for Tayside House, the 17-storey office block completed in 1976, which soon acquired the nickname of 'Fawlty Towers.' Bus services were dispersed around the city centre. One side effect was an increase in car parking charges to 10p per day for all-day parking in designated blue areas, and 20p for five hours or 5p for a short stay in red areas. Car drivers also had to suffer the almost continual roadworks associated with the inner ring road. Although proposals for this had been first mooted in 1952, it was a further 28 years before the final £4 million phase, Allan Street and a tunnel

This panoramic view from the Dallfield multis shows the progress of the Wellgate development in November 1975. To the left is St Andrew's Church with the road bridge in the background. (Evening Telegraph, Dundee)

The Hilltown and town centre from the Derby Street multis in May 1971. (Evening Telegraph, Dundee)

under Victoria Road, were completed. The Tay Bridge landfall area was overarched by ungainly pedestrian walkways to serve the new developments on the riverfront and the Tay Bridge railway station.

There were new buildings outwith the central area. The ultra-modern three storey Western Fire Station at Blackness Avenue costing £500,000, with a 60ft drill tower, was built in May 1960 and was joined in November 1972 by the smaller Kingsway East Fire Station at Craigie. Barnhill shopping centre opened in November 1971.

The regeneration of Lochee in 1976 proved controversial. The new shopping centre in the High Street and the supermarket built behind it replaced many traditional shops and many felt the underpass was grim, dark and a source of danger. One resident, a local business man, declared 'Lochee has been murdered'.

The position of the Overgate as Dundee's premier shopping centre was seriously challenged in 1976 when the covered Wellgate Centre opened. In May 1979, the opening of Wellgate Centre Market Hall was a further body blow. The Market Hall leased to 70 small traders closely resembled the popular arcade or even Dens Road market. While the rest of the Wellgate fought for the upper and middle sectors of the retail market, the Market Hall attracted the lower budget sectors. The writing was on the wall for the Overgate.

The Wellgate Centre has proved popular with shoppers since its opening in 1976 and the pedestrianised Murraygate is one of the main shopping areas. (A.M. Scott)

Left: The Wellgate Centre top floor looking across the central atrium. (A.M. Scott)

Right: A good place for a natter with a customer. (A.M. Scott)

Heading into Industrial Downturn

In the early 1970s Dundee's industrial estate was the second largest in Scotland, with a total 1.5 million sq ft of factory floor space (after Hillingdon which had 4 million sq ft) and a workforce of 15,000. The success was due to its excellent layout, the first-class locations of the factories and the availability of a large pool of labour. In 1972 Levi Strauss arrived in Dundee and set up a jeans factory at Kilspindie Road. In October, a £750,000 headquarters for William Lows was opened at Dryburgh industrial estate by George Younger, Secretary of State for Scotland.

But NCR – the giant on the Dundee scene – was in trouble. The company had had a dramatic rise as Dundee's largest employer, with nine factories and 6,500 employees. But decimalisation had required an unrealistically high level of employees. The company had failed to realise quickly enough that the electronic age would be less labour-intensive. In 1971 the company issued redundancies to 1,200 workers, followed by a further 800 in June 1975, and in September 1976 600 more were out.

The most spectacular event of the decade was the jute fire at William Halley's on 3 March 1979. There had been an eight-day battle with a jute fire at Lower Pleasance in June–July 1976, but this was the most spectacular blaze in the city for decades. Significantly, it was also the first involving

polypropylene. Seventy firemen battled the blaze in the three-storey building
for 24 hours, some on a hydraulic platform. In all they used 10 pumps, and
two turntable ladders. 'This was a major emergency,' said Alfred Jones, Tayside
firemaster. Firebrands started fires as far as a mile away. This included a paint
shop at 170 Albert Street, which became a secondary blaze. At one point, a
100-foot section of the factory exploded into Arthurstone Terrace. Residents
from seven tenement closes in Erskine Street were evacuated, a total of 100
people, and accomodated in Buists' Spinning Mill in Dura Street. In all, one
and a quarter million gallons of water were used. The damage was estimated
at £1 million. It was 'like the aftermath of the Blitz,' according to the
firemaster.

Dundee and Oil

The first licenses for sea-bed exploration in the North Sea had been issued in
1964 but it was not until the first oil from the Forties field began to flow in
1975 on a pipeline opened by the Queen and Energy Minister Tony Benn MP
that things started to happen. The British National Oil Corporation was
founded in 1976 and four years later, Britain was self-sufficient in oil. From
the first it was known that the Scottish oilfields were a high-cost production
area but the subject of oil, how much of it there was and who should benefit
from it, was a highly emotive issue. Aside from these political questions, the
popular myth is that Dundee lost out to Aberdeen as 'oil capital' through some
lack of effort or poor planning.

Information from secret government files in 1971 released in 2002 shows
that it was Dundee's, not Aberdeen's, harbour which was considered most

modern and easiest to adapt to the needs of the oil industry, and it was accessible in all tide states. The Dundee Harbour Trust, with the Corporation Planning Department, sent a brochure out to all industrial firms in the area extolling its available industrial space, its convenient airport, good water supply, communications and engineering expertise. The planners wanted Dundee to copy Great Yarmouth, the boom town of North Sea gas and oil, the Houston of the gas fields which within seven years had attracted 93 companies to set up in the town. In October 1972, Dundee Chamber of Commerce sent delegations to Great Yarmouth and also to Lowestoft, Grangemouth, Aberdeen, Montrose, Methil, Cromarty and the Moray Firth to see what would be required in Dundee to facilitate market opportunities. It was estimated that there were 100 Dundee men working in North Sea oil developments in 1972 compared to 1,000 in Aberdeen, but BP publicly admitted that it would have to spend £500,000 building facilities in Aberdeen which were already available in Dundee. Prospects looked good. Dundee sent three service ships regularly to the oil rig *Sea Quest*, and by August 1972 this had risen to nine. BP suggested that 23 of its oil supply ships might soon use Dundee.

The news in January 1973 that Aberdeen planned £500,000 investment to make its harbour usable around the clock and add a new graving dock came as a blow to Dundee's hopes, but Dundee fought back by developing an additional 540ft of modern quays at the Eastern Wharf for oil service boats. In January a new oil storage tank was built for Dundee Petroseas Ltd. A 40-year-old Texan, Arch Bell, with a wide knowledge of the oil business and good connections, was appointed manager. Within days, a huge new oilfield discovery was made by Occidental 100 miles off Wick, north of the Forties fields. This was the Piper field. Even bigger finds were soon made and these were in 500ft deep stormy seas, but crucially, being further north, they favoured a pipeline landfall and servicing at Aberdeen. Dundee did not give up. In September 1975 they took the fight to Aberdeen with an eye-catching display at Offshore Europe '75. 'We are serious challengers for increased offshore business in North Sea and worldwide,' said a spokesman. One year later, the city seemed to have accepted it had lost the lion's share of the business in a report by the Port Authority:

> Although no North Sea oil is landed at Dundee or is likely to be in foreseeable future, thousands of tons of liquid gold for use on rigs and production platforms is shipped out by a Dundee supply fleet. Only one drilling rig, the Norwegian owned *Havdrill* has visited Dundee but two recently completed giants the *Dundee Kingsnorth* and *Kingsnorth UK* are registed at Dundee, also the *Oil Hunter*, a seismic survey ship.

Oil led to expanding activities at Kestrel Marine – barges with scrap steel from the Claymore field arrived, also tugs for repairs and a ro-ro Blue Star liner for engine repairs. The Port Authority reclaimed four acres at Stannergate for future development.

Oil news stories, with dramatic pictures of rigs, heaving seas and blowout stacks became a familiar sight on TV screens. Ministers were under political pressure from the SNP and Liberals to divert the revenues into a Scottish Oil Investment Fund. The issue had particular relevance to Dundee because Dundee East MP Gordon Wilson was a frequent expert commentator on the subject, the originator of the SNP's emotive and highly successful 'It's Scotland's Oil' campaign. Labour saw its support ebbing away and frenziedly counter-attacked. After decades of claiming Scotland was too poor for independence, they now claimed that keeping income from oil revenues in Scotland would be selfish. The oil issue was central to the Dundee East by-election of 1973 and the two general elections of 1974.

Comprehensives, Colleges and Libraries

In May 1970, Princess Alexandra had opened the £1 million Dundee College of Commerce, which had a student roll of 4,000 students. In March 1972 the foundation stone was laid for Dundee College of Education's new campus at Gardyne Road. The new campus, which would allow teaching and social work students to transfer from the Scrymgeour Building in Park Place was a 29-acre site expected to cater for 1,800 students, 200 staff, 70 non-academic staff and 100 part-time staff. It would be October 1975 before the college opened. At a cost of £4 million, it was second only to the Overgate in terms of scale. It took one year alone to solve drainage and foundation problems.

More schools were opening: in August 1970, Craigie High School 'the first purpose built comprehensive school in Dundee', costing just under £1 million; then exactly a year later, Menzieshill School opened. It was in fact a 'twin' of

An aerial view of the 'Skarne' blocks at Whitfield, which no doubt gratified the architects (if no one else!) in 1978. (The Courier, Dundee)

Kellyfield Primary School, which opened in April 1974, was another of the open-plan schools constructed in the area. (Evening Telegraph, Dundee)

'I don't wanna go to Whitfield!' snarled Dundee punks Bread Poultice & The Running Sores in the 1970s. Faceless, anonymous, drab, 'Gulag' Whitfield was widely believed to be a punishment colony for the unemployed, single parents and the elderly. (The Courier, Dundee)

Craigie High School and like Craigie its swimming pool would be open for community use. In 1973, a second Roman Catholic secondary, St Saviour's, opened with an initial roll of 650, mostly from Craigie High. In August 1976, Whitfield High School, which had taken four years and £2 million to plan and build, opened under the headship of Peter Murphy. Unusually, it had no assembly hall – instead, like Whitfield Primary and Kellyfield, there was a multi-purpose area. Children at Whitfield and Fintry could now have their entire school education in their home area.

The library service was expanding to the peripheral areas. In June 1971 Duncan Torbet, the chief librarian, attended the opening of Kirkton branch 16 months after Menzieshill branch. In July 1973, Broughty's library extension was open for business. In 1978, the long-awaited move of the Central Library from the Albert Institute to the new custom-built premises in the Wellgate went ahead. Then contractors got to grips with the worsening problems in the foundations. In the Wellgate, the library attracted a surge of new members and the Steps cinema and new conference facilities gave a boost to the city's educational aspirations.

Housing Issues and Problems

As early as 1972 Whitfield was being described as 'the great Dundee housing idea which has gone sour'. There was increasing reluctance to move there,

Logie Secondary School pupils about to board the SS Uganda *for a two-week holiday cruise in June 1973. The liner operated from 1963 with up to two trips a year from Dundee.* (The Courier, Dundee)

even among tenants on the waiting list. There were various reasons for this. It was the most remote housing scheme and also the largest with 4,800 dwellings and a projected population of 11,000. It was expected that it would finally wipe out Dundee's house waiting list, but 300 remained empty with some 200 still to be built. Even when tenants were found the turnover was rapid. The area degenerated. Vandalism and gang trouble, particularly at the shopping centre, intimidated the elderly. The perception of a high crime rate (not borne out by the statistics) and publicity afforded to the problems of the area did not help attempts to form an organic community.

In October 1970 the Revd Hugh C. Ormiston laid the foundation stone for Whitfield parish church, which, completed by spring 1971, served the largest parish in Dundee, some 22,000 parishioners.

Not all of the scheme was problematic. The south part, off Whitfield Drive, consisting largely of semi-detached dwellings, was popular. The problem was most acute in the northern half, where 2,500 Skarne dwellings in a honeycomb of 130 separate blocks, which had cost £8.5 million, were sometimes known as 'the barracks'. These layers of maisonettes with deck access were crammed in at 60 per acre. This was high density housing. Between each group of five blocks was a 'no-man's land' of grass and drying greens which often became a muddy swamp unsuitable for children to play on. Everyone was overlooked by everyone else and yet this only increased the sense of isolation. Noise echoed around the scheme. This was an instant slum.

One of the most problematic areas was Dunbar Crescent, later known as Moonlight Alley – which broke records for the number of tenants who vanished from it leaving considerable rent arrears. In less than a year 50 families did a 'moonlit flit' from this street alone, 10 percent of the city's 'bad debtors' total in 1971. Eviction notices pasted on doors became a commonplace sight yet the debts were typically between £20 and £60. The City Factor was forced to write off £28,000 that year and that did not include rent owed to the Scottish Special Housing Association or private landlords, nor repair or cleaning bills. In Dunbar Crescent and other streets in northern Whitfield, 150 rented TV sets went missing every year, the highest number of any Scottish city and the electricity and gas companies began to operate stringent credit checks on addresses in the area. The problem was mainly one of young families inexperienced at dealing with budgets and unable to plan their household expenses.

The Corporation's Housing Study 1969–70 resulted in the shelving of the remainder of the Skarne-type dwellings, and at Kellyfield 300 low-density cottage-type houses were built. A valuable, if costly, lesson had been learned. In March 1972, the Wellgate housing scheme was a deliberate step back to central area housing with 308 houses, all with living rooms facing south or west and with covered parking areas. It was awarded a Saltire Commendation in 1979 one of few ever awarded in Dundee. The Corporation also made strenuous efforts to provide residential homes for the elderly. In 1972 there were six and six more were planned by the new Social Work department, set up in 1970 to provide 'cradle to grave' care, which already employed 800 staff.

Healthier Prospects

'A Technique Used In Space Now Makes Operations Safer' and 'Carparks Are Cleaner Than Operating Theatres!' were the headlines in the national press after Dundee bacteriologist Dr Charles C. Scott revealed a new system of laminar-linear airflow ventilation for mobile or standard operating theatres. Based in the university medical school, Dr Scott demonstrated a £1,500 model operating theatre in a disused warehouse at 150b Perth Road to senior medical staff from across the country. Filmed on BBC TV's *Nationwide* programme, the system virtually eliminated bacterial particles in the air which normally led to as many as one in 10 operation wounds turning septic and the public was invited to see 'the space age operating room in action' on 19 November 1971.

Further up the Perth Road, at Ninewells, the gigantic new hospital was nearing completion and stirring controversy with its costs destined to top £22 million, double the project estimates. The hospital finally admitted its first patients in January 1974, three years and six months late. It was, according to the late George Hume of the *Scotsman*, a 'monument to misdirection, delay and fortuitous involvement'. Delays had cost an extra £5.5 million and it was revealed that the contractors, Crudens, had been paid £1.7 million damages

Workers leaving the Robb Caledon Yard at lunchtime, September 1979. (Evening Telegraph, Dundee)

for delays they had themselves caused! 'The project has,' reported Hume, 'caused the Scottish Office a lot of worry.'

The initial estimates in 1951 had been below £2 million. The local MP, Peter Doig, took up the issue of the professionals' fees. It seemed that these, based on a percentage share of the contract, offered a major reason for procrastination and were already topping £2 million! Other things were going wrong; defective linings in chimneys, gas leaks, problems with air conditioning (which only existed in the operating theatres), visitors getting lost in the corridors (including the famous mile-long corridor). There were allegations of doctors using skates to get around, problems with catering staff, complaints that the digital clock system had never worked. The elderly were complaining about long treks to the wards. There were allegations of a lack of security, hardly surprising with a payroll of 3,200 employees of all types, 40 telephone lines and 1,200 separate extensions. And there was the urban myth of the bulldozer bricked up somewhere into the foundations. Of course the new hospital was not the accident and emergency centre – that was still the DRI – and this caused some confusion. But Ninewells was the first completely new teaching hospital built in the UK this century and it gradually began to get the better of the criticism by the sheer scale and quality of its output. It became a centre of excellence with a worldwide reputation, conducting 12,000 operations in its first year. In January 1975, simultaneously at 7am, the maternity department at DRI closed and the spacious new midwifery services unit opened at Ninewells.

Demoralised DRI staff were fed up of being asked when their hospital was to close. In fact, in 1976 some £160,000 was spent on improvements in accident and emergency, four areas of specialist surgery and two general medical wards, and the total was brought up to over £500,000 in the next few years. The DRI also gained a new department – renal dialysis.

In February 1976 some 'spratters' still operated from Camperdown Dock. (The Courier, Dundee)

Social Diversity and the Rise of Leisure

Decimalisation of the coinage occurred on D-Day, 15 February 1971. For months, the public had been helped to prepare for it with displays about the new coins. The idea was that after D-Day shops would decide which currency to use. In the event, the change-over was easier than anyone had predicted and within weeks, everyone was using the new coinage exclusively, although there were widespread allegations of 'rounding up'. For most, the new coins were lighter and more convenient. You could buy a loaf of Milanda plain or pan for 9p, standard eggs were 21p a dozen. A tape of Leonard Cohen's *Songs of Love and Hate* cost £2.39, the Rolling Stones' *Sticky Fingers* album was £2.25 from Chalmers & Joy's two outlets at 79 Hiltown and 9 Albert Street. Posters of Jimi Hendrix, Roger Daltrey, Joni Mitchell, Elvis Presley and Steve McQueen would set you back 60p each. The rent for a three-room flat was on average £3.20 per week, electricity might cost £1.25, a week's food bill might come to

Dens Road market in September 1972. It was highly popular as a meeting place and retail outlet for second-hand goods for many years. (The Courier, Dundee)

Mrs L. Whyte, Mrs G. Hancock and Mrs H. Reid having a blether at the café in Dens Road market in February 1971. (Evening Telegraph, Dundee)

The Dundee ice rink's Saturday morning sessions were popular with teenagers as this picture taken in January 1975 shows. (Evening Telegraph, Dundee)

£5 plus HP payments of £1.50, with 60p for the bingo, so most had money to spend on leisure pursuits.

Shops were busier because of the legislation allowing six-day shopping and making the half-day closure mandatory. One of busiest shopping centres was the City Arcade under the Caird Hall, which had entered its fifth decade. This cornucopia of small shops and stalls with wares hanging and displayed around open doorways and by the counters included Puckel's fancy goods store and Agnes Hynd's amusement stall, with its fruit machines and rides where you could get a 6d ride on anything from a koala bear to a rally car, although you had to buy the sixpence until the slots were converted to take tokens. Other popular shops were Imrie's fruit and flowers; the Radiant Health Centre – one of the oldest health food shops in Britain; Sam McLeish's fish and grocery store; Mitchell's of Letham with its game hanging on hooks and roasting chickens; Phil Soave's Fruit Mart; John Roy, fruiterers; George Ray, butchers; the Gift Shop; Campbell's children's wear; prize bingo and an amusement arcade developed in 1972 by Colin and Alex Hynd, which offered the latest in one-arm bandits. The lucky winners could take home vouchers for sheets, or packages of cold meats, chairs, lamps or bathroom sets. There was also the

Interior of the City Arcade in August 1973. (The Courier, Dundee)

ultra-modern records and fancy goods store, Cathie McCabe's, with its octagonal counters to display LPs and tapes. Cathie was one of the arcade's cheeriest characters.

Other popular leisure activities included indoor bowling at the indoor bowling rink in Miln Street, which was the second largest in Britain with a turnover of 400 players a day. Pigeon racing had been popular for a decade and the Dundee Federation of Racing Pigeon Societies had eight clubs.

In May 1972, Dundonians were having trouble with wildlife. A plague of mice was reported in Jamaica Tower, Alexander Street. The baffling thing was

The Dundee Highland Games in Caird Park were popular events for all the family. The picture shows Lord Provost Harry Vaughan and the Lady Provost with spectators in June 1977. (The Courier, Dundee)

The legendary George Kidd bids an emotional farewell to the crowd in the Caird Hall on 2 March 1976 after winning his final wrestling bout against Steve 'Iron Man' Logan with a double leg nelson in the third round. After 30 years in the ring and more than 1,000 fights, only seven of which he lost, the 51-year-old was retiring undefeated after 25 years as World Lightweight Champion, having successfully defended his title 49 times, a career record unlikely ever to be equalled. (The Courier, Dundee)

that mice were reported on all 21 floors, and in the lifts. About 40 had been killed by residents, by poisoning, being thrown out of windows or hit with sweeping brushes. The tenants held 'mouse-killing championships'. The rodents had obtained entry by the water pipes and ascended 200ft.

Over in Peddie Street in April 1973, a group of young squatters had set up a community in semi-derelict property whose Bermuda-based owners had gone bankrupt. This was the Touch group, based at 66 Peddie Street, whose members claimed supplementary benefit, although Tony Stark, their self-elected leader, ran a left-wing bookshop in Corso Street. With Yvonne Marshall, who described herself to the *Scotsman* as an 'active woman's libber', they formed a tenants association and set up the West End Association community newsletter. Members of the group included Bob and Pam Carroll and 'Ann,' an unemployed former art school model, stripper and go-go girl who 'now spends her time reading four library books a day.' Legal action was taken against a tenant at No.58 under the 100-year-old Trespass Act but 'one feels that the action of Tony in laughing in court can't have done much to elicit sympathy,' the journalist reported. He was arrested for contempt of court but later released. 'Don't call us a commune...' he pleaded, 'yes, we know people think we are lazy, idle and so on, well there are 10,000 unemployed in this town so there aren't any jobs to get.' The community in Peddie Street and Annfield Street was to swell to several hundred over the next two years and included many of Dundee's radical youth and musicians.

There was live music to suit all tastes in the city. The Taybeat competitions in the Palace Theatre in 1963 elicited entries from hundreds of local musicians and was won by local group Black Diamonds. In 1973, a five-piece jazz rock band called Elegy won the *Melody Maker* contest and later teamed up with US singer and pianist Sharon Taber for an American tour. The Wally Dugs were the resident group at Dundee's new folk club in the Nine Maidens. Kindred Spirit were the resident band at the Glencarse Hotel – most had been members of the Chalet dance band before it was renamed Sands. The Jimmy Deuchar Quartet, formed in 1972, did a weekly set at the Sands, while the legendary East Coast Jazzmen were at the Invercarse. The Tayside Jazz Action Group worked to bring big names to Dundee. Other working bands included Exhibition (Stan an de Liver), the Sleaz band, Sundance, later renamed Diamond Lil, Staccato Five and, towards the end of the decade, the soul band Mafia.

On 20 May 1977 an excited crowd of more than a thousand pushed and jostled the Queen and Prince Philip during their walkabout at Camperdown Park on the third day of the Silver Jubilee tour. On Tuesday 24 May, as the Queen and Prince Philip drove down the Hilltown, he suddenly turned and pointed at the Windmill Bar. The staff and customers were curious about this and sent the Duke some verse about the incident. To their surprise, he responded in verse. The poem was framed and hung in the bar and led to worldwide interest.

In March 1979 an application by the Central Council of British Naturism to allow nude bathing on Monifieth beach was discussed by Dundee District

Blowing up a storm! The East Coast Jazzmen, founded in the 1950s from 'trad' sessions at the Dundee Jazz Club and still playing festivals 50 years later, seen here in their 'dance band' phase, in residency at the Invercarse Ballroom, c.1968. (Left to right) Jimmy Wallace, Ron Elder, Dave Fimister, Andy Tully, Harry Morrison, Les Cameron and Dave Moodie. (Harry Morrison)

One of the most popular bands in Dundee in the mid-1970s was Skeets Bolliver, which regularly played Thursday night sessions at Laings Hotel, Roseangle. The line-up here is (left to right) Chris Marra, Gus Foy, Pete McGlone, Brian McDermott, Michael Marra and Stewart Ivins. (The Courier, Dundee)

A 'hippie wedding' at Dundee Registrars, Commercial Street, February 1970. (Evening Telegraph, Dundee)

Council. 'The whole idea sounds daft. They'll freeze to death' claimed Councillor Ian Mortimer of Monifieth East. The application was turned down on the casting vote of the chairman of Dundee District Recreation Services Committee – and the members of the committee kept their clothes on.

Dundee's social life had long encompassed gambling in various forms. The Chevalier Casino in the Seagate had operated since 1972, playing roulette,

Moira McGovern (19) and Lynne Bruce (20) were among the hostesses at the new-look Barracuda in July 1978 which featured live music and dancing for the over-21s and a drinks licence until 2am. Guest artistes included Mac and Katie Kissoon, Rokotto, The Marmalade, Ray King and the Flamingoes and Limmie & The Family Cooking. (Evening Telegraph, Dundee)

blackjack and operating a variety of gaming machines. It was joined in 1974 by a second Reo Stakis-owned casino, the Thistle, which in 1979 was renamed the Regency. The casinos attracted a wide range of customers and were popular with Dundee's Chinese community. Sometimes £5,000 could be won on a single spin of the wheel. In March 1978, Tayside

Regional Council set up its own lottery which became the most successful of its type in the UK and offered 3,000 prizes every week, from 50p to £1,000. Each week 60,000 tickets costing 25p were sold. In one year it made £200,000 for the council, which was spent on wheelchair ramps, uniforms for Tayside Police Pipe Band, and a bus for Anton House mentally handicapped centre, while some 50 percent was spent on tourism and recreation projects.

Dundee United capped a successful season in December 1979 by lifting the Scottish League cup. The final at Hampden against Aberdeen resulted in a nil-nil draw and was replayed at Dens four days later on 12 December, when the Tangerines won 3-0. Exactly one year later, McLean's men repeated the feat, this time against local rivals Dundee, whom they beat 3-0 with goals by Davie Dodds and two by Paul Sturrock.

The Barracuda (on the site of the former JM Ballroom which closed in 1974) had opened in May 1975 and its exotic south-sea islands theme, created by owner Murdo Wallace junior, owed a lot to the Disney film 20,000 Leagues Under The Sea. It was sold to Rank Leisure in 1980. (Evening Telegraph, Dundee)

Gang Violence and The Mone Murders

In the early 1970s there were at least eight teenage gangs operating in the city, causing mayhem, particularly in the city centre at weekends. These included

The famous Dundee landmark, Wallace's Auld Dundee Pie Shop, a bakery and tearoom which had opened in 1927 at 22–24 Castle Street, after an earlier incarnation in the Vault since 1892, closed in April 1977. Once known as the haunt of councillors, 'the pie shop parliament' may have been the site of the shop of James Chalmers, the inventor of the postage stamp. (The Courier, Dundee)

Dorothy Dobson, Dundee University's assistant director of PE with her exercise class for 6 to 60-year-olds at Hawkhill Sport Centre, April 1977, which from the first received a staggering response from the public, particularly among the over-60s. In 1992, Dorothy was Citizen of the Year and in 1999 was awarded an MBE. (The Courier, Dundee)

Linda Lavery of Fintry Road won the Hoover Miss Dundee Playhouse Beauty title in July 1970 and went on to the Miss UK finals in Blackpool. Second was Helen Reynolds (left) of Charles Street and third Linda Young of Perth. The event was staged in Green's Playhouse, Nethergate. (The Courier, Dundee)

the Lochee Fleet, the Toddy (Douglas and Angus) the Hula based in Honeygreen, the Hilltown Huns, the Fintry Shams, YMB (Young Mary Boys), Ardler Park and the Mid, and this was considered by police to involve a total of perhaps 500 boys between the ages of 14 and 19 and also girls of similar age. By far the largest were the Fleet with up to 200 known adherents. There were frequent clashes in Caird Park involving a multitude of weapons and these were pre-planned events. The Kirkton Huns, the first gang formed, dissolved when the Kirkton community centre opened. John P. Gray, the Procurator Fiscal, believed gangs had sprouted in the three years from 1969–72. 'Until then mobbing and rioting charges were unheard of in Dundee.' Gang graffiti began to appear on walls throughout the city, including the Overgate walkways.

One of the most appalling crimes of the decade was the murder of eight-year-old Sharon Smith of Broughty Ferry Road on 21 May 1971. The child had been taken for a ride on a Lambretta scooter by 24-year-old Charles Shepherd, who knew her parents. She was discovered in the grounds of Linlathen House after a two-day mass search. She had been raped and her throat had been slashed with a razor. Shepherd received a life sentence. In August 1972 retired antiques dealer Leonard Pollington, 73, was brutally attacked in his flat in Seafield Road, West End, and died of a stroke three hours later. Four men from Hamilton were later convicted of the crime but this type of incident in Dundee was rare. Apart from the gangs, the other main problem which Tayside police had to deal with was the drugs menace. In December 1973 the CID had a list of 400 names of known drug offenders, users of cannabis and LSD, although there was as yet no evidence of heroin in the city. Underage drinking by school pupils led to the setting up of the Prohibition Squad by the chief constable. The school age population was 11,600 and it was estimated that there were approximately 400 regular underage drinkers. There were a total of 299 liquor outlets in Dundee at that time and the police strength was 385, indicating the difficulty of the problem which was exacerbated by the fact that pupils over the age of 14 were allowed by law to BE in licensed premises but not to drink alcohol. The under age drinkers' favourite drink was strong lager, while rum chasers were the favourite of underage girls. With teenagers' increasing fashion consciousness and use of makeup, it was almost impossible for publicans to guess their ages.

On 20 February 1979, Robert Christopher Mone (52) of 93 Glenprosen Terrace was charged with the brutal murders of three women in a house in Kinghorne Road and also with two breaches of the peace, three assaults and a theft charge. Other charges included sexually-motivated assaults on two men. Mone had strangled the women, Mrs Jane Simpson, Miss Agnes Waugh and Mrs Catherine Millar over the Hogmanay and New Year period in a drunken spree. The son of a lamplighter, Mone was short, barely five foot five, and heavily tattooed. He appeared in Dundee Sheriff Court in a grey suit and orange sweater. The Crown cited 98 witnesses and some of the evidence related to a silver ring with a green stone which belonged to Mone's son. Mone junior, being unable to wear it in Carstairs, had sent it to his father. The ring was to prove a crucial piece of evidence, directly linking him to the murder of two women, for it had made distinctive imprints in their skin. He had visited his son just after the murders, allegedly to relate the grisly details of the killings. The jury took 75 minutes to reach their verdict. They were entirely unaware of his 40-year record of serious violence, dishonesty and drunkenness. He had received jail terms in 1942, 1946, 1953 (twice), 1956 and 1960, for serious assault and robbery. On 5 June 1979 Mone was sentenced to life, with a recommendation that he serve a minimum of 15 years. Mone showed no flicker of emotion. He stared at Lord Robertson. 'Would you mind backdating it, eh?'

It was reported that Mone showed powerful emotion towards his son. He said he longed to be with him. He visited his son just after the murders were committed. Before the crime he said he was going to make a name for himself. He had revelled in every detail of his son's break-out from Carstairs in

'Steamies', or
Corporation-run public
wash houses, remained
popular from their
inception in the early
1920s into the 1970s,
long after the advent of
launderettes and mass-
produced domestic
washing machines.
(Evening Telegraph,
Dundee)

December 1976, nine years and one month after the murder of Mrs Hanson,
when, with another inmate, Thomas McCulloch, he hacked an officer to death
with an axe, killed a patient who tried to stop them and escaped over a
perimeter fence using a rope ladder. They faked a road accident and when a
policeman stopped, he too was axed to death. The chase lasted 70 miles to just
north of Carlisle and included assaults and the taking of hostages in a lonely
farmhouse. Lord Dunpark described their activities as 'the most deliberately
brutal murderers he had dealt with… dangerous and incurable psychopaths.'
To Mone senior, his son was the 'Carstairs Killer' and he boasted that he would
do better. He had worked on and off as a jute spinner. His employer testified
that he often worked as hard as two men, yet his neighbours had taken a
petition to the Housing Department about him, claiming he terrorised them.
Mone senior met a violent death in prison in January 1983 at the hands of
another inmate.

In 1979 another crime was to achieve notoriety as the 'largest murder
inquiry ever conducted in Dundee.' On 27 March, police extended the six-day
manhunt for the killer of Carol Lannen (18), whose nude body was found at
10.30am on Wednesday 21 March by a dogwalker. Carol had been picked up

The old spin-driers at Logie wash house in 1967. The wash house in Logie Avenue opened in 1923 and closed in 1951 to re-open in 1953 as one of the first modern all-electric steamies of its day. But customers preferred elbow grease to automation and the machines were removed and replaced by handwashing stalls. (The Courier, Dundee)

in the Exchange Street area on Tuesday 20 between 8 and 9pm. Twenty-five officers combed the woods to no avail. The trail had gone cold but was to be reviewed less than a year later with the discovery of a second body in Templeton Woods.

The Trojan Wars

Thomas Moore had been elected Lord Provost in May 1973 after a spell as Housing Convenor. His company Trojan had been previously investigated but cleared by Labour's National Executive in a row about land deals. At 47, Moore was one of Dundee's youngest Lord Provosts. Within weeks there was controversy over land deals although he had agreed to suspend these during his term in office. It was 'The Dundee Dossier' programme on ITV's *World In Action*, an hour-long investigation of the

Dundee fans of Elvis Presley held a memorial ceremony at Our Lady of the Sorrows Church, Fintry, in August 1979. (The Courier, Dundee)

conflicts of interest and house-building contracts and demolition work done by Trojan Plant for Dundee Corporation in the 1960s, which stirred up the issue again. Moore had declined to be interviewed in the programme which was screened on 15 April 1975.

Tom Moore was the son of a shoemaker. His mother died when he was four. On leaving school he worked for 12 years as a jute clerk and in 1957 was elected for Ward 10 (Douglas) having two years previously become the chairman of the city Labour Party at the age of 29. Within six months of being on the Corporation he faced the first of many controversies. The Housing Committee considered letting ground to his wife for a lock-up garage in Fintry. The Tenants Association complained that the ground was earmarked for a playpark. In 1959 he contested Perth and East Perthshire, coming bottom of

Lord Provost Tom Moore leaves City Chambers moments after his press conference on 5 May 1973 under pressure from the media. (The Courier, Dundee)

the poll. In the meantime he had a family of six. He bought a newsagents for £50 which he sold nine months later for £800. He bought the Alhambra Garage, Monifieth, the Tay Bridge Garage and Macalpine Motors. He sold these and moved into the licenced trade, buying a pub in the Hilltown, then expanded into bookmaking and then into property. In 1965–6 he was investigated by the police, and questions were asked in Parliament as a result of which he lost his convenorship of the Housing Committee. This was the 'Evans case', when he allegedly put pressure on the City Factor to allocate a council house. In 1965 his company, Navarre Properties, applied for a hotel licence for a six-bedroom hotel on the site of a demolished factory in Old Glamis Road. The application was opposed by Chief Constable John Orr, who claimed the hotel would have the largest drinking area in the city, with room for 1,000 drinkers, yet only six bedrooms. The licence was refused and an appeal at court was lost. Then JPs alleged they had been approached on behalf of Moore at the appeal. 'The whole thing stinks' ex-Bailie Andrew Wallace said. It was alleged Moore had approached John Maxwell, a joiner who had become manager of a firm of shop fitters, to influence the three JPs. A special meeting of the Labour Party accepted his denials. In 1972 Trojan Demolition had a turnover of over £1 million, with up to 80 machines for hire.

A major proportion of demolition work in and around Dundee related to Corporation projects such as major road works, sewage schemes and the construction of sea walls. Moore hired out much of his plant equipment to the Corporation Public Works Department. His peak year was 1973, when he was employing 250 people and acquired a second chauffeur-driven Daimler. The TV programme turned up other interesting aspects of Dundee's redevelopment: the Lord Provost had led delegations to get the go-ahead for the Wellgate Centre (demolished by Trojan, built by Crudens); the Town Clerk negotiating for a 180-acre development site found out 'overnight' that he was dealing with Crudens who later got the £11 million contract. There many other unexplained coincidences.

Several days after the 1975 *World In Action* programme, the General Committee of Dundee city Labour Party failed to expel Moore, Harry Dickson and James Lumsden Stewart by the required two-thirds majority. The Scottish Executive sent a three-man delegation which decided that no action should be taken. Stewart, a former Housing Convenor, had 30 years of membership and attacked the '*nouveau gauche*', claiming it was a left-wing group which had raised the expulsion move. It was true that a left-wing faction was gradually assuming power and from the late 1970s used many means, including a weekly newspaper the *Dundee Standard,* to consolidate their power, but in 1975 they were as yet only a faction. Bailie Dickson had been in the party for 35 years including 21 years as a councillor. Moore's 'crimes' related to 'irregularities in Council matters... he had not declared interest when he should have,' relatively minor matters, Moore claimed. But public pressure built up. Gordon Wilson MP invited Willie Ross, Secretary of State for Scotland, to come to Dundee, since 'there was a need for wide ranging inquiry into the local government of the city'. By contrast, Peter Doig MP described the case as 'trial by television'. By 29 April, the president of the Chamber of Commerce was complaining that the 'good name of Dundee was being dragged through the mud.' With local government reorganisation looming the three were cold-shouldered in May 1974, not reselected as candidates and finally expelled. In 1976, Stewart was one of two bailies acquitted of bribery and conspiracy charges concerning not sending three men to prison, but he, Tom Moore and John Maxwell were due for trial on major corruption charges, postponed because of the illness of Maxwell.

Confrontations and Decisions

The early 1970s was a time of serious political strife. The three-week-long Miners' Strike led to a State of Emergency and the 'Three Day Week' and in 1973 there were several confrontations in the North Sea in what was dubbed the 'Cod War' with Iceland. Local politics meant intensely bitter contests.

   The retirement in 1973 of George Thomson, Labour MP for Dundee East since 1952, triggered a Dundee East by-election. Labour's candidate George Machin brought in the big guns, Michael Foot MP, John Smith MP, and many leading councillors, while activists from across Scotland and some celebrities came forward to help the SNP, including larger-than-life folksinger Hamish Imlach. A mysterious new splinter party from the SNP, the Labour Party of

The new MP for Dundee East, Gordon Wilson, celebrates his victory by sharing a kiss with his wife Edith after the declaration in the leisure centre, 28 February 1974. (The Courier, Dundee)

Scotland, was formed and put forward a candidate. In the event, Labour scraped home with a majority of slightly fewer votes than the LPS candidate, George Maclean, had gained. The LPS mysteriously disbanded shortly afterwards.

In the general election of 28 February 1974, the SNP's 35-year-old solicitor Gordon Wilson won Dundee East with a majority of nearly 3,000 on an 81.8 percent turnout on a bitterly cold day. Peter Doig retained Dundee West for Labour, although in a second general election, on 10 October 1974, the SNP's Jim Fairlie cut Peter Doig's majority to just 2,802 votes and Gordon Wilson increased his majority to just under 7,000.

The SNP debated whether to contest the local elections. The debate, in second-floor offices at 23 Panmure Street, was acrimonious. With a large number of ambitious activists, the party might have gone straight into forming an administration, but it was felt that the prospects of holding Dundee East could be hindered by the difficulties untried and inexperienced councillors must face in the glare of publicity. The decision was a huge reprieve for Labour and with hindsight, a classic blunder. With nothing to do for four years, activists melted away and the party shrunk to the single task of defending its hold on Dundee East, allowing Labour to move all its big guns to the east. When Gordon Wilson was overwhelmed – although, against the odds, he held on until 1987 – the SNP collapsed like a house of cards.

The Wheatley Commission proposals ended the Dundee Corporation and in May 1974 created Dundee District Council, one of 53 Scottish district councils and Tayside Regional Council, one of nine regional authorities. Although Dundee had voted heavily for Labour candidates in district and region, the Conservatives from Angus and Perthshire had a majority in the new Tayside Regional Council which met in the new Tayside House tower. But it was an Independent, Duncan Miller, who became chairman after a cut of the cards with Progressive leader William Fitzgerald.

After Labour's troubles with the 'Moore Affair' the selection of Charles Farquhar, the councillor for Lochee East, as Lord Provost of the newly reorganised Dundee District Council in May 1974 was unexpected. Labour hoped that it would allow them to draw a line under the debacle. However, on 13 October 1975, Lord Provost Charles Farquhar

Former Paisley solicitor Gordon Wilson served as MP for Dundee East from 1974 to 1987. National Convenor of the Scottish National Party for 10 years, he was the founder of the successful campaign and slogan 'It's Scotland's Oil'. (The Courier, Dundee)

William K. Fitzgerald, the former master butcher and businessman who at one time owned 11 shops and a wholesale bakery in the area, served as Dundee's Lord Provost from 1970 to 1973. In 1975 he lost out on a cut of the cards for the post of Tayside Regional Council's first convenor, an office he assumed in 1978, when he also became president of COSLA. (Evening Telegraph, Dundee)

Lord Provost Charles Farquhar in 1978. (Evening Telegraph, Dundee)

was convicted, after a day-long trial, of assault on a van salesman called Byres who had taken part in the Camperdown Open Golf Tournament on 19 July 1974. The victim required 23 stitches after Farquhar had allegedly 'put the head on him' twice, although Mr Byres had clearly offered considerable provocation. Farquhar's solicitor put in an appeal. In the meantime there was a furore, with petitions raised both calling for him to resign and expressing support for him. The council considered the matter several times and Farquhar instigated a police inquiry into two Conservative councillors. The matter dragged on and in mid-February 1976, the council voted 31 to 11 for his immediate resignation as Lord Provost after his court appeal had been rejected. At the meeting on 16 March 1976, which had attracted unprecedented public interest, with seats being provided for the first time on the floor of the chamber itself to accommodate the demand, several members refused to stand when the Lord Provost entered. He made a three-minute speech in which he declared that he had no intention of resigning and that the trappings of office, the chain, TS1 the official car and his allowance were legally his until his term of office ended in May 1977. This astonished the council and the meeting ended in uproar on his words: 'I rule the resolution out of order and declare the meeting closed.' The Lord Provost was snubbed by Dundee Business Club, whose president declared 'Dundee cannot afford to be associated with a Lord Provost who brings disrepute upon our city,' and prevented from attending various foreign trips, but the affair blew itself out and he regained the support of the Labour group.

Although Farquhar has been at the centre of controversy on occasion since, the whole affair was the only blemish on a lengthy career of continuing public service for which he was awarded an OBE.

Dundonians went to the polls on 6 June 1975 to vote in Britain's first-ever referendum. The turnout was 63.8 percent, less than in the general elections, partly due to disinterest in the subject of Europe. Tayside voted 'yes' to continuing EEC membership by a margin of 105,728 votes or 58.6 percent to 74,576 or 41.4 percent. There was a second referendum on 3 March 1979, when the Callaghan Labour Government proposed the Scotland Act with the notorious Cunningham amendment requiring 40 percent support to make a 'yes' result binding, which in effect meant that dead persons on the register and those who did not vote were voting 'no'. Labour and SNP ran separate 'yes' campaigns. The 'Scotland Says No' and 'Scotland Is British' camps had large funds and the support of many prominent Labour MPs. In a nail-biting count at the Caird Hall, Tayside narrowly voted 'no' by the narrow margin of 1,843 votes. While 93,325 had voted 'no' the 'yes' votes totalled only 91,482, on a turnout of 63.15 percent. George Galloway believed Dundee had voted 'yes' but that 'fear of SNP-type separation had scared the voters elsewhere in Tayside.'

Peter Doig, Dundee West MP since 1963, retired at the age of 65. In his 14 years in Parliament he was mostly known for his Guard Dogs Bill. 'Harold Wilson and Ted Heath laughed their heads off at it but I was once a bakery salesman and I know what it's like,' he said, 'for the thousands of postmen who have to face the menace of unruly dogs.'

In 1979, the Labour Government of James Callaghan collapsed and Mrs Thatcher arrived at No.10 promising that 'where there is discord we shall bring peace.'

The Tayside Region Structure Plan '76–86, which appeared in 1979, suggested the city's population was falling. By 1986 if trends continued, a population of only 189,000 was predicted, 5,500 less than in 1976. All other Tayside areas had an increasing population. (See *Appendix, Figure 2*) Unemployment was expected to rise and attracting new industry was, as ever, the main priority.

John Reid examines a euphorbia in the glasshouses at the Botanic Gardens. Located in 26 acres and with over 2,000 plants on display, the gardens opened fully to the public in July 1977 after six years of opening by arrangement to students and schools and are one of the city's most delightful and restful spaces. (A.M. Scott)

CHAPTER 5

The Unequal Eighties

The Battle for Robb Caledon

Only six years after the centenary in 1974, when Dundee's shipyard workers had looked back with pride at the 500 ships which had slid down the slipways into the Tay, a desperate battle was underway to save the Dundee yard. International over-capacity and a lack of demand had led to empty order books. The Thatcher government was disinclined to prop up nationalised 'lame ducks' and after eight months of anxiety and rumour, voluntary redundancy packages were offered. Bob Barty, convenor of the Shop-Stewards Committee of the Confederation of Shipbuilding and Engineering Unions, was 'greatly disheartened by the rush' to take these up in May 1980. Two hundred accepted but the remainder fought on to save the yard. In June, a delegation from the city comprising Lord Provost James Gowans; Councillors Charles Bowman and Jack Watson; the city's MPs, Ernie Ross and Gordon Wilson; Harry McLevy, former yard convenor and now area secretary of the engineering union; and Alex Allan, a steward from the yard, met British Shipbuilders' bosses in London.

On 19 October 1981, 140 Robb Caledon workers began a sit-in after BS announced that 'the yard had lost £12.8 million since nationalisation and is losing £250,000 a month and had been unsuccessful in obtaining work... there is no alternative to closure.' Bob Barty believed there was a dirty tricks campaign to orchestrate the closure of the plant. The men particularly resented the allegation of restrictive practices and demanded an investigation. This was conducted by a BS industrial director, who 'could find nothing in the existing local agreements or in existing practices which could possibly account for the low performance of the yard. On the contrary, it appeared that (they) were well in advance of the rest of the industry.' The unions collected productivity data and allegations of poor productivity were never substantiated by BS. As for the claim of losses, it was later admitted that only £2 million of a £14 million loss was attributable to the Dundee yard, yet BS, claimed the workers, made no effort to correct the impression that had been given. It was this kind of manipulation of the facts that particularly angered Bob Barty. 'They are confidence tricksters. I could never sit with them again and believe a word they say.' He had been at the yard off and on for 40 years, served his time there, and being quite apolitical, became a union leader 'by accident' in 1978. He had been in on all the discussions, including a 12-hour meeting in Blackpool. Like the rest of the men, he suspected that attempts to find work were a cosmetic exercise. Not a single order had come through for the yard although the men were willing to accept any kind of work no matter what its scale, size or nature. The union had documentary evidence of scores of inquiries inviting tenders for jobs, yet not one tender had been won, the main reason being that the 'Dundee design office was fully occupied' doing work for other BS yards. There were also claims that other tenders had been switched to Leith.

Harry McLevy paid tribute to the 140 men who spurned the opportunity of cheques of between £1,800 and £13,000 and the prospect of work with Kestrel Marine, which offered shorter hours and better pay, to fight what he described as 'voluntary compulsory redundancies', a battle which was finally lost. The final ship to roll down the slipways was the 2,996-ton MV *Koscierzigne* in 1980, although a 62ft ferry, *Tyne Countess*, tiny by comparison with normal Caledon orders, and built entirely in a shed, was launched on 11 May 1981.

...and elsewhere on the docks

Kestrel Marine, the fabrication and repairs yard at Prince Charles Wharf, which gained some workers from Robb Caledon, was expanding into the

The first ship to leave Dundee harbour from the roll-on roll-off ferry terminal was the Angus *in 1980.* (The Courier, Dundee)

The RRS Discovery, *strapped within a cage on the deck of the support vessel* The Happy Mariner, *returns to her home port of Dundee in 1986. Thousands turned out on both sides of the Tay to watch her lap of honour.* (F.J. Scott)

repair of offshore oil modules and had, in 1984, some £30 million-worth of contracts in hand. Tristar Oilfield Services, oil well head and drilling specialists, having started with six employees in 1986, were by the end of the decade at the leading edge of North Sea technology, with 31 employees, leading the UK's charge in the new markets of Nigeria.

1985 was a black year for the city with the liquidation of Dundee Ferries, a brave joint venture between the Dundee Port Authority and the Bibby Line of Liverpool, after losses of more than £1 million after only six months of trading. Three weeks earlier, on 3 December, the ferry had run aground in a Force 10 gale in the Tay estuary and that proved symbolic. 'We just did not get the sales… people were loathe to change their methods of transportation,' said a spokesman. 'The hauliers did not want to use us until we were firmly established and we could not get established unless they used us.' Less than half the predicted turnover of £1.5 million was achieved. From the outset there had been an imbalance, with many more customers coming over from Rotterdam than going out from Dundee. Eighty percent of business came from European companies. Scotland's first roll-on, roll-off freight link had been a brave attempt, doomed by a lack of enterprise among over-cautious local businesses.

In an ironic twist, exactly one year after the final ro-ro ship left Dundee, another ship, the support vessel *The Happy Mariner* entered the Tay on 2 April 1986 bringing, strapped on its deck, the wooden-hulled RRS *Discovery*. This historic vessel's return was watched by thousands from the north bank of the river and was increasingly to be used as a symbol of civic regeneration.

Dundee Projects

In the last decade 10,000 manufacturing jobs had disappeared from Dundee. The city changed more drastically in the 1980s than in any other post-war decade. There was an underlying sense of vulnerability but by the end of the decade a greater sense of confidence and a revival was based firmly on funding by the regional and district councils and the Government through various support organisations. Dundee became an Enterprise Zone in January 1984 and was also a Special Development Area, and in November 1982 the Dundee Project was initiated to allow collaboration of the two councils and the Scottish Development Authority, which would invest £18 million over three years. Tayside Region invested £6 million and planned to attract another £16 million of private investment.

On the industrial scene, carpet manufacture had ceased and jute had almost disappeared. There was some good news; small new companies such as Davy Offshore, WL Gore, Shield Diagnostics and Dunclare Dispensers had arrived.

In the last three months of 1983 Timex workers broke production records with an early computer, the Sinclair Spectrum. It was the end of the era of large payroll employers because Timex had originally employed 4,500 and now had less than half that number. Over at NCR, there was something of a renaissance. They had started the decade threatened with closure and were to end it as world leader in high-tech automated teller machines. At Ferranti it was industrial lasers and while the famous name of Keillers & Sons might have disappeared in the early days of the decade, the new owners of the Kingsway factory, Okhai Ltd, had invested £20 million in the company including £5 million in a bottling plant at Wester Gourdie. The chairman, Ibrahim Okhai, had arrived from Africa and started a trading group in the mid-1960s. With his brother, a St Andrews medical graduate, Dr A.A. Okhai, they started selling torch batteries and built an £8 million turnover from lollipop sticks, flexible packaging and commercial stationery.

Dundee was already expanding into high-tech industries and the electronics sector. But optimism that a major new manufacturing company was coming to the Dundee industrial estate was deflated with an unseemly row over union recognition. The refusal of the unions, especially the TGWU, to let the AEU agree a single-union deal at the new Ford plant led to some extraordinary statements, not least from Ron Todd, general secretary of the TGWU, when he arrived on 9 April 1988 and refused to meet anyone except his TGWU branch officials and Lord Provost Mitchell, a TGWU member. There was widespread outrage in the city at the unions' behaviour and many Dundonians signed a

An aerial view of Whitfield in August 1980. (The Courier, Dundee)

In 1988 David Jones, a 22-year-old Abertay University student, founded DMA Design, whose first video game Lemmings was a worldwide success. It was followed by other games including Grand Theft Auto. After buying back his own company in 2001, he set up Real Time World and relocated back to Dundee. (Alan Richardson photography)

Dundee's airport is owned, uniquely, by the City Council, and almost shut down when Business Air, which operated flights to Manchester, was swallowed up by British Midland. A new operator, Suckling Airways (now renamed Scot Airways) arrived in the mid-1990s and the airport now handles an increasing number of passengers on its London routes. (A.M. Scott)

petition. On 25 March 1988, the headlines said it all: 'Dundee Despair as Ford Says No!' It was the farcical end to the 'Ford fiasco', for the £40 million electronics plant and its 450 jobs relocated to Portugal.

One of the principal themes of the Dundee Project was to redesign the central waterfront, but this was dogged by public distaste for the lack of imagination of the plan when it was put on display for the public to see. More than half a mile long, the front was to be taken up with Tesco, a DIY superstore and 1,000 car parking spaces. There was to be a cinema – without any windows facing what had been described as the best estuary frontage in Europe – but Mecca Leisure pulled out in 1989 after Cannon and Rank had already done so and UGC Cinemas was 're-assessing its position.' There was criticism of the three existing modern buildings on the front: the swimming pool complex, described by one respondent as 'like a power station', Tayside House, widely known as 'Fawlty Towers' and the Earl Grey Hotel – 'a breeze block with windows'. The public hated the walkways, the degeneration of the rail station and the fact that the river promenade was effectively cut off from the town. The 2,000 visitors to view the original plans were virtually all critical. In September 1989, the design of the £48 million development was criticised by the Royal Fine Art Commission and 13,000 signed various petitions against it.

In September 1980, Air Ecosse introduced a new 65-minute service to Manchester. Although the aircraft was only a 17-seater, this was an important milestone after five bleak years when the city had been without regular air connections. The regional council backed the scheme for the only municipal airport in Scotland to copy Bristol, Leeds and Luton in England and it was

hoped to achieve passenger numbers of 9,000 per year once the service was established.

The city fumbled its opportunity to create a bus-rail transport interchange terminal at 'Site 6' on Enterprise Zone land to the rear of the railway station. The bus station at Seagate was more than 1,000 steps away from the railway station and travellers faced an assault course of six roads, including three busy junctions, and two flights of steps or ramps to cross. There was also the secondary question of the appalling run-down state of the bus station and the public conveniences – heavily vandalised and therefore often closed. Faced with the opposition of Scotrail, the regional council bought the site to seek an ice rink operator, but the Enterprise Zone land finally ended up as offices for the Inland Revenue and HM Customs.

One good news story was the 1980 opening by Grampian Television of an electronic studio at Albany House in West Ferry. This had an electronic news gathering unit, and was the first TV station to use lightweight portable cameras and video cassettes, thus enabling more TV coverage of Dundee events by its assiduous local reporters, Alan Saunders and Ron Thompson. The BBC studios were in Dock Street.

'The Enemy Within': Dundee Politics in the 1980s

In early 1980, the newspapers were full of the details of the long-delayed trial of former Lord Provost Tom Moore, James L. Stewart and John Maxwell, which had been transferred to the High Court in Edinburgh to counter the risk of bias against the defendants. The three were found guilty of corruptly soliciting rewards and using influence to ensure that the Wellgate Centre was built by Crudens. They received jail sentences of five years but Moore and Maxwell appealed and were freed. Since the trio had been expelled from the Labour Party in 1975, the public might have felt that Labour had cleaned up its act in Dundee, and as the decade started, things could not have looked better. A membership of 3,000 in the 1950s which had declined to 450 by 1970 had climbed to 1,500 in the 1980s partly due to the rise of the left within the party. Moreover, in May 1980 Labour swept to power in Dundee district with 25 of 44 seats to the Conservatives' 18. But it was a very different Labour administration which now took power, for all but three were left-wingers. The leader, George Galloway, a 25-year-old, had failed to be elected despite standing in the safe Labour seat of Gillburn. It was alleged this was because he had alienated Catholic voters by living 'in sin' with his fiancée. Despite not being elected, Galloway was in an unassailable position as secretary/organiser of the party, being answerable only to the party's National Executive who had appointed him in 1977.

George Galloway had been born in Lochee and was something of a rebel at Harris Academy. He had begun plotting to overthrow the Labour heirarchy in the city in the early 1970s with a small group who booked rooms in the name of the North East Debating Society and met in pubs such as Ross's or the Royal Hotel. By the elections of 1980, Galloway was described as 'the absolute ruler of Dundee… a new-style city boss… his rise has been meteoric, the stuff of political stardom.'

The new council immediately caused controversy with its refusal to sell council houses even when ordered to do so by the Secretary of State for Scotland. No Labour councillor bothered to attend a packed meeting in the YMCA on 23 May 1980, attended by 250 tenants, leaving the unelected Galloway to defend the council decision. They raised the combined regional and district rates by 150 percent (the steepest rise in the UK). They called an emergency debate over the Craig Owl radio installations, which they alleged to be bugging their telephone conversations. They antagonised the Royal British Legion and Burma Star by their plans for lighting a beacon on the Law war memorial to the dead of Hiroshima.

The most controversial policy was the twinning with the West Bank town of Nablus, the stronghold of the Palestine Liberation Organisation. In September 1981 Colin Rennie attended the International Conference of Solidarity with Lebanese and Palestinian People in Beirut, and in March the Lord Provost, James Gowans, and three councillors, Colin Rennie, Ken Fagan and the Independent councillor Ian Mortimer, made a prolonged visit to facilitate the twinning arrangements. The delegation was met in Amman by CBS and ABC TV crews and reporters from *The Times* and *The Guardian*. The twinning had created worldwide controversy. The Arab newpaper, *Al-Fajr*, devoted a full page to the visit under a headline 'Dundee The Most Popular Town In The West Bank After Nablus'. Councillors Rennie and Fagan 'clarified the press background for *Al-Fajr*: "The *Courier* is actually anti-Jewish but they dislike the Labour Party more so the 'near-hysterical' attack on the twinning was expected."'

Less impressed was the small Jewish community of Dundee, whose synagogue was attacked and daubed with swastikas and anti-semitic graffiti. Four hundred protestors, led by Greville Janner MP and Gordon Wilson, collected signatures on a petition in the City Square in February 1982. The city suffered numerous attacks over the Nablus affair including a 10-minute election broadcast by John Cleese for the Social Democratic Party which described the city as a 'looney-left' citadel. Nablus remains one of Dundee's twin cities although the arrangement is more symbolic than real. If it seemed that the new administration was more interested in striking postures, evidence that they were also interested in power was demonstrated by the 'Labour Clubs affair'.

There had been Labour Clubs before; at Roseangle where the 200-strong, all-powerful General Management Committee met to decide policy and the Dundee East Labour Club at Rosebank Street, but when a club opened in Whitfield on 1 December 1978, followed by Ardler the following December, both had substantial waiting lists, and by 1981 the Whitfield Club had a turnover of £250,000. George Galloway and others saw the potential of the clubs as a source of funds and a place for councillors and activists to be seen in their communities and build up their profile and disseminate propaganda. The clubs were tightly controlled by a small coterie of trusted councillors and officials and there was a stipulation that no one could be elected onto the committee without five years of Labour Party membership. More clubs were set up; the Dundee West Labour Club in Camperdown and, controversially, in 1982, a club in Menzieshill. At the Earn Crescent site a local group had toiled for over two years to secure the backing of Scottish & Newcastle after Drybroughs pulled out and had built up a membership of 475 members with a waiting list of 300. Despite their prior claim to the club, the Labour-controlled council supported the application from Menzieshill Labour Party. Galloway neatly diverted the focus of the debate by claiming that the local group had 'turned their committee into an SNP front', which was hotly denied. There was an outcry and appeals to the Scottish Secretary, the Home Secretary and the ombudsman, but the Labour Club went ahead. After four troubled years, however, it closed with huge debts. But in June 1982, Galloway was boasting that the four new clubs were making an annual turnover of over £1 million. How much of all this money was siphoned into the coffers of the Labour Party or the pockets of its councillors will never be known because in December 1982 someone poured petrol through the letterbox of the Labour Office in Rattray Street and set it on fire. Residents in the flat above the offices managed to escape but the accounts of the Labour Clubs for 1978–82 were, it was subsequently claimed, destroyed in the blaze. In 1983 George Galloway left Dundee to take a job with War on Want, where he was pursued by claims of profligacy with his expenses.

In February 1983 Dundee East Labour Club at Rosebank Street closed for refurbishment and never reopened. Menzieshill closed in October 1986 and Ardler in December 1986, owing more than £200,000. The cashbook had pages torn out and more than £30,000 was missing. In 1988 Roseangle closed and Camperdown went into receivership. Where had the money gone? The police began a painstaking investigation into the clubs.

On 6 November 1986, Channel 4 showed the documentary *In The Red* as part of their *Dispatches* series. Made by STV over a lengthy period it considered numerous allegations about the clubs, 'bounced' cheques and Labour officials such as Councillor Ken Fagan, who, in June, had been elected president of COSLA. *Private Eye* had remarked that this was like making Al Capone the mayor of Chicago. Other allegations concerned Councillor Philip Grubb. A story had appeared in the *Sunday People* claiming that the married father of two had been having an affair in a council flat at Duart Place, Trottick, and that money was being regularly taken from the till at Whitfield Labour Club to pay the tenant of the flat so that Councillor Grubb could have liaisons with his mistress on an inflatable bed. He was alleged to be one of the people benefitting from free drinks at the club. Later his house was broken into and his set of keys to the club was apparently stolen. Subsequently, £4,000 was found to be missing from the club safe. Councillor Grubb hit the headlines again in 1994 when he was convicted of his third drink-driving offence and banned for 10 years.

Labour were hit by more scandals in the 1980s but with the departure of several left-wingers, the party moved more into the 'mainstream left' so that Mary Ward, a 31-year-old teacher and the first woman leader of the council in May 1986, was soon disillusioned enough to defect to the Communist Party and stand against Labour in the mid-1990s.

The deepening crisis in the South Atlantic in early 1982 revealed the human drama of a pregnant Dundee woman trapped in the beleaguered Falklands. Mrs Veronica Fowler, the daughter of Mrs Mary Gibson of Kenmore Terrace, had lived in the Falklands for 13 years. Her husband John was head of the Education Service. While normally islanders would attend hospitals in Argentina, would that be possible, they wondered, if there was a war? The baby boy was born in the midst of the crisis but later Veronica and John were gravely injured when they were hit by a stray shell.

Dundee service personnel were heavily involved in the Falklands War and some, such as Jim McGinnis, 26, whose parents lived in Eskdale Avenue, West Kirkton, were injured. McGinnis, who served in the Royal Engineers Commandos, was hit by shrapnel in an Argentinian bombing raid in San Carlos, East Falkland. Dundee seamen who were on HMS *Sheffield,* which suffered a direct hit, survived and four Dundee men on the merchant ship *Atlantic Conveyor,* which was sunk by Argentinan missiles, also survived. RAF

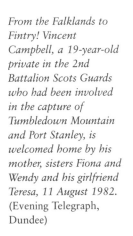

From the Falklands to Fintry! Vincent Campbell, a 19-year-old private in the 2nd Battalion Scots Guards who had been involved in the capture of Tumbledown Mountain and Port Stanley, is welcomed home by his mother, sisters Fiona and Wendy and his girlfriend Teresa, 11 August 1982. (Evening Telegraph, Dundee)

Squadron Leader George Penman, acting as air controller with the paras, received a leg injury at the Battle of Goose Green. Two other Dundee paras of 2nd Parachute Battalion, Anthony Banks and Stephen Gormley (20) who received a leg injury, were in the final push to take Port Stanley. After the Argentinian surrender on 14 June 1982, several parties were held in Dundee to welcome servicemen home on 12 July. Paras Banks and Gormley were given a heroes' welcome at the Masonic Halls in Park Street and the return of two other paras, Raymond Hind (22) of 3rd Para, whose family lived in Mid Road, and Robert Taylor, was celebrated at GJ's pub in Mains Road with cake and flags.

The predominant theme of politics in the 1980s was strife and division, exemplified in 1984 during the prolonged eight months of the Miners' Strike in Mrs Thatcher's notorious phrase 'the enemy within'. The introduction of the Community Charge or 'poll tax' as it was universally known in April 1989 in Scotland (a year ahead of England) created the main political battleground for several elections. Political activists, including the new Scottish Socialist Party, formed from various left-wing groups, led 'non-payment' campaigns and some held public burnings of poll tax books in City Square. While a large majority were opposed to the charge the numbers who refused to pay or delayed payment rendered it uncollectable and created massive debt problems for Tayside Regional Council and the Sheriff Officers they employed to collect arrears.

Mrs Thatcher, the 'Iron Lady' – something of a hate figure in Dundee – made her first and only visit to Dundee on 6 September 1989, to be shown around James Keiller's confectionery factory. Poll tax protestors awaited her

Dundee's Pakistani community hold a ceremony at the Wellington Street mosque, June 1987. (Evening Telegraph, Dundee)

and in an interview with a local reporter she was less than delighted to be reminded that the Conservatives were standing at only 16 percent in opinion poll ratings in Scotland. The staff at Keiller's were disappointed that Mrs Thatcher made no attempt to taste the sweets and she hurried, clutching her handbag, to complete her itinerary by opening a new business premises for Alma Holdings.

Inquiries Are Continuing

The decade started with the shocking discovery in February 1980 of the near-naked body of Elizabeth McCabe in Templeton Woods, only 150 yards from where Carol Lannen's body had been found 11 months before. A nursery nurse in her early twenties who lived with her parents in Lyndhurst Avenue, Clement Park, she had disappeared after attending the Junction 9 Disco at the Tay Hotel. She was also known to frequent Teazers' Nite Club in Union Street. Police questioned disco-goers and pursued the search for two cars; a red Ford Escort and a blue Austin Princess. A Dundee Appeal Fund was set up by friends and fellow disco-goers for information leading to the capture of the killer. This was to reach almost £5,000. A top-level CID conference, headed by Detective Chief Superintendent James Cameron, head of Tayside CID, was called to

Some of the runners at the start of the Dundee Marathon, 24 April 1983. (The Courier, Dundee)

consider the two murders and possible links with the murders of Christine Eadie and Helen Scott in East Lothian in 1979 and three other women who had last been seen in discos in Strathclyde. The discovery of this second body restarted the original inquiry and over 1,000 interviews were conducted. On 27 August 1980, a red Ford Escort which had been stolen from Whitfield Avenue two weeks before was found abandoned at Burnside of Duntrune. Inside were newspaper cuttings from the Lannen and McCabe murders.

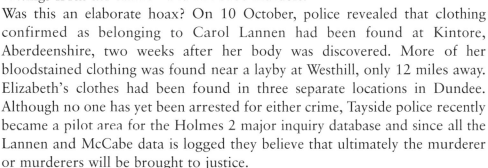

Was this an elaborate hoax? On 10 October, police revealed that clothing confirmed as belonging to Carol Lannen had been found at Kintore, Aberdeenshire, two weeks after her body was discovered. More of her bloodstained clothing was found near a layby at Westhill, only 12 miles away. Elizabeth's clothes had been found in three separate locations in Dundee. Although no one has yet been arrested for either crime, Tayside police recently became a pilot area for the Holmes 2 major inquiry database and since all the Lannen and McCabe data is logged they believe that ultimately the murderer or murderers will be brought to justice.

Runners finishing strongly at the end of the Dundee Marathon, cheered by crowds in the High Street. (The Courier, Dundee)

Comfort was provided to competitors at the hospitality tent in City Square. (The Courier, Dundee)

The May bank holiday in 1980 was the hottest in living memory, three long days of sunshine. Men strolled around the city centre stripped to the waist and young women in bathing costumes stopped traffic. The buses to the beaches were busy and crowds sunbathed at Castle Green or swam in the sea. Broughty Ferry was like the Riviera, with the colourful spectacle of yachts and speedboats, but the weekend ended with three more murders in Dundee. The third victim was June Kelby, 48, of Midmill, who had been killed by her ex-husband, but the perpetrator of the gruesome double murder at 2 Roseangle was never publicly charged with the crime. The victims were Dr Alexander Wood and his wife Dorothy. He was a well-known retired doctor, the former chairman of Dundee Executive Health Council, an invalid with an artificial leg. They were last seen by their son, a GP in Aberdeen, who left the house at 5.20pm on Saturday 17 May. Some university students playing football at Seabraes had climbed over the railings into the garden to retrieve the ball and glimpsed the bodies through a basement window. They had been dead for 24 hours, murdered with an axe. Police issued a description of a photographer seen in the area on the day of murder – but this man came forward and was discounted. Another man with a suitcase – dark blue morocco leather – was never found. Nor was a door-to-door 'professional scrounger'. More than £2,000 of jewellery, silver, coins, watches and a clock had been stolen. Even local criminals were sickened and offered to help. The police saturated the West End and pursued various leads about cars seen in the area but the case petered out, apparently unsolved. However, according to Detective Superintendent Norrie Robertson of Tayside police, a man called Henry Gallacher who was subsequently arrested and convicted for the brutal double

Council workmen remove 60 tons of salt which had been used as mock snow during filming of An Englishman Abroad *in February 1983, starring Alan Bates as Guy Burgess. The Caird Hall, in the background, had served as the Bolshoi Theatre and more than 70 locally hired extras played a theatre audience. Housing Convenor John Henderson, who had 'looked terribly Russian' was persuaded to play a role as a KGB driver in greatcoat and traditional fur hat.* (The Courier, Dundee)

murder of a priest and a housekeeper in Yorkshire had been in Dundee at the time of the Roseangle murders and had even written a book about himself in which he gave details of the Dundee crimes. 'He suffered from Crohn's Disease, and had left very obvious proof of his whereabouts in Dundee. You could say we were hot on his trail. He was the subject of a report but the case never went to Court. As far as we are concerned, the case is closed.'

On 1 March 1988, a Broughty Ferry man stood accused at the High Court in Stonehaven of murdering his wife. William Crowe (58) of Strathbeg Place had allegedly pushed his wife Mona off 100ft cliffs at Arbroath on 1 September 1985. The six-foot tall silver-haired businessman denied the charge. At first the death had been treated as a tragic accident. Crowe convinced everyone he was a grieving spouse. His wife's insurance was routinely paid out within weeks of her death. He then told relatives he had to make a new start and after travelling to the Philippines on 22 December, brought over June Casayuran, whom he subsequently married. The relationship foundered when neighbours told her what had happened to Mona. She found the death certificate and, suspecting what had happened, moved out, but did not report her misgivings to the police. The trial came about by complete accident when she was contacted by immigration authorities about her legal status. She told them why her marriage had broken up. The CID was called in and Crowe was arrested.

Much of the trial evidence related to a letter Crowe had sent to Orient Introductions, a dating agency, claiming he was a 47-year-old divorcee. The

prosecution claimed the letter had been sent seven months before the death of his wife, thus proving premeditation. Forensic tests conducted on it proved that the date had been altered from three months before Mona's death to three months after. The photographs which he had sent with the letter were of Dundee in summer and not winter as he had claimed. Crowe had subsequently married a second Filipino girl, Emelita (28), but on 9 March 1988 was given a life sentence for murder.

Two events in the summer of 1989 shocked the city. The body of Gordon Johnston was found in Gow's Gunshop, Union Street, by police at 5pm on 8 May. The popular manager, who had 33 years service, had been attacked in the shop soon after opening. Guns had been stolen. The crime was re-enacted on BBC's *Crimewatch* three weeks later and two 21-year-old men received life sentences in August. Three weeks later and only 100 yards away, two armed men raided the West Port branch of the Bank of Scotland and terrorised staff into giving them £2,000. The culprits were later apprehended.

St...stayin' Alive!

In January 1981 Gordon Wilson had opened the Wishart Centre for the homeless, in what was formerly the Wishart Memorial Church, and later revisited the third of an acre of empty space at the rear of the building which was converted into a 'City Farm'. This urban smallholding set up with funding from the Manpower Services Commission employed a Community Services volunteer and four Youth Opportunities Scheme youngsters and became an off-the-beaten-track visitor attraction with its pigs and goats, rabbits, geese and ducks, not to mention tiny patches of rye, wheat and a midden. The manager, Colin Forrest, believed that the project would have educational benefits and there was an element of proselytising for a more organic lifestyle. Not everybody in Dundee was obsessed with industrial output or inward investment.

A very different kind of campaigner was Paul Phillips or Spring (31), the owner of a sex shop in Strathmartine Road. The police had raided the premises and seized £35,000 of material. He claimed to have 2,000 members and declared he would open again but he did not. Dundee's sex trade in whatever

Left: RRS Discovery *and the custom-built quay and Discovery Centre.* (A.M. Scott)

Right: RRS Discovery *has proved a popular tourist attraction and potent symbol of the regeneration of 'The City of Discovery' since her return to the city in 1986.* (A.M. Scott)

Former St Saviour's pupil Liz Lynch does a lap of honour after winning a gold medal in the 10,000 metres at the Commonwealth Games in Edinburgh, July 1986. As Liz McColgan she went on to win another gold in 1990 and narrowly missed out at the Olympics in Seoul in 1988 before winning marathon races in London in 1991 and 1996 and New York in 1991, staking her claim as the greatest female long-distance runner Scotland has produced. (The Courier, Dundee)

guise, like its prostitution, has generally been almost invisible to those unaware of its existence.

Unexplained events in a Fintry House in 1981 led to an exorcism being performed. The Gorthy family of Finlow Terrace, terrified of noises and strange happenings and the sudden freezing of rooms called in the Revd James Powrie, who prayed in every room after agreeing that the house was the scene of demonic activity. This appears to have done the trick! But more mundane disappearances were also causing consternation. On 19 June 1981 it was announced that the Odeon, which had been, since 1909, the Hippodrome Theatre, King's Theatre, King's Cinema (1928) and the Gaumont (1950–73) was to be closed by its owners Rank. Generations of Saturday Morning Club members were disappointed. Others recalled concerts by Cliff Richard, Billy Fury, Georgie Fame, Joe Brown and many other stars. In its day it had hosted hundreds of films and plays, concerts and live opera national touring companies.

Theatre in Dundee has not had an easy time in the 20th century but many were anticipating a boom when the Rep moved to their new custom-built building in Tay Square. A fire in 1963 in Nicoll Street had led to the theatre company moving to a succession of temporary homes including a tent in Camperdown and for some years an old church in Lochee Road. Prospects improved when Dundee University gifted land next to Tay Square Halls in 1973. But inflation made new building too expensive. For a time it looked as if the Rep might fold entirely. They hoped to obtain the old College of Education in Park Place but the faculty of law had a prior claim. In January 1978 a public appeal was launched and in autumn when it looked like construction work might begin an objection by a local resident caused delay. The plans had to be altered to move the building's frontage back 12ft. Principal Drever cut the sod on February 1979 but the alteration had increased the cost by £300,000 to a total not far short of £1 million, causing a huge gap in funding. Another public appeal raised £60,000 – a remarkable achievement in a city of high unemployment – then a £20,000 anonymous donation and an interest-free loan enabled the work to go ahead. There was a further dispute with subcontractors, but on 8 April 1982 the Rep re-opened with a production of John Heggarty's *Tonight We Celebrate* starring Angus Lennie, known to many as 'Wee Shughie' of ITV's *Crossroads*, which, quite appropriately, told the story of theatre through the ages.

On 18 May 1982 there was a silent protest outside Orchar Gallery in Broughty Ferry as the £1 million art collection of 400 paintings was removed to storage premises in Dundee. The bequest, by former Broughty Provost James Guthrie Orchar, carried the stipulation that the paintings were for display in the gallery in Broughty Ferry. Although there was never a risk of the old burgh seceding from Dundee, the Orchar Action Group with the support of Dr James McIntosh Patrick were incensed and largely supported by residents who campaigned for their return.

In March 1984, the Dundee Rockets were attempting to retain their British

Champions title. Despite their lack of a home ice rink, the Rockets were the undisputed kings of British ice hockey under the coaching of Tom Stewart, who had played for the old Dundee Rockets before the sport died in the mid-1970s. In the late 1980s, Dundee Whalers catered for the increasing interest in American football.

In March 1988, the BBC began filming *Christabel*, a Dennis Potter drama. Parts of Dundee had been doctored to resemble wartime Berlin. Dundee High School was festooned with Hitler hoardings and made to look like the Reichstag, while areas of Lochee and the Camperdown works were selected because they looked as if they had been flattened by bombs!

On 7 July 1988, the world was shocked by the oil rig disaster on Occidental's Piper Alpha platform which was to be the biggest news story of the decade. Of the 167 dead many were from the east of Scotland. One of the 67 survivors was instrument technician William Young of Fontstane Place, Monifieth. He had clambered down the leg of the blazing rig into a rescue boat. 'I realise I am a very lucky man,' he said. Another survivor was John Menzies of Americanmuir Road, who had been asleep in the accomodation module when the rig exploded. For 20 minutes he and another Dundee man had been trapped in a drill shed before the shed collapsed on them. He leaped

Erected in 1890 and listed in 1986, the Magdalen Green bandstand was doomed until the West End community council's campaign to save it raised £14,000 from the public over four years. With a grant from Dundee District Council and the proceeds from the auction of a MacIntosh Patrick watercolour, the bandstand was saved. (A.M. Scott)

A spectacular night picture of Dundee Rep in Tay Square. (Alan Richardson photography)

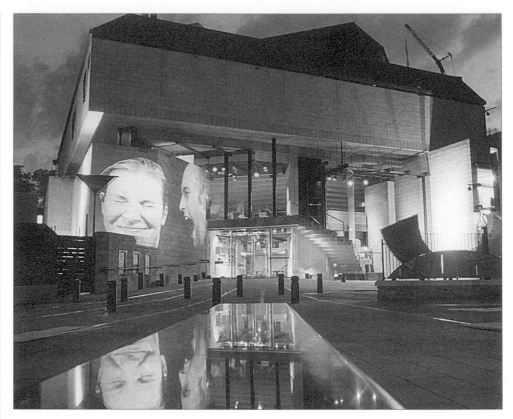

150ft into the sea, swallowed a lot of oil and suffered extensive burns but was hauled aboard a rescue craft. For days, relatives hung on in hope that there might be more survivors. Some bodies were never recovered. The Dundonians who died included crane operator William Duncan of Hawick Drive, Craig Barclay of Park Avenue, Frederick T. McGurk of Fintry Drive, chief steward Alexander Duncan of Dalmahoy Drive, Harold Flook of Fotheringham Drive, Monifieth, Alexander Laing of Portree Avenue, George Murray and John Goldthorp of Carnoustie and many others from Angus. Altogether some 16 Tayside families were bereaved and there had been four survivors from the region. Craig Barclay's fiancée told of a phone call 48 hours before the tragedy in which he said that he had refused to light his welding torch because he smelled gas. A safety inspector had corroborated his claim at the time and this information was passed to the inquiry team. Dundee set up its own North Sea Disaster Fund which collected donations through local banks. Tayside Regional Council donated £25,000.

A Menzieshill man, James Clark, was at the centre of the rescue effort underneath the blazing rig on the specialist standby rescue vessel *Silver Pit*. He helped to rescue 30 men before his own vessel was badly damaged by fire. He was later awarded a George Medal, one of five presented by the Queen at Buckingham Palace in March 1991.

On 22 December 1988, a Dundee lorry driver gave a first-hand eye-witness account over his cellphone of the devastation when the Boeing 747 of PanAm flight 103 exploded above Lockerbie. Keith Osgood, a driver for PS Ridgway

The famous five at Tannadice, 10 March 1987. (Left to right) Bannon, Holt, Kirkwood, Hegarty and Sturrock. (The Courier, Dundee)

Dundee United manager Jim McLean and Gundar Bengtson, coach-manager of IFK Gothenburg, before the second leg of the UEFA Cup final at Tannadice in May 1987. (Evening Telegraph, Dundee)

Paul Sturrock takes the field at the first leg of the UEFA Cup final at IFK Gothenburg's Ullevi stadium on 6 May 1987. (The Courier, Dundee)

United players at the end of the game, having lost 1-0. Although the second leg was a 1-1 draw and the Tangerines' cup hopes were dashed, Jim McLean commented 'my players gave every ounce they had'. (The Courier, Dundee)

Haulage was on his way from Lancashire to Dundee on the A74 and was less than a mile away when the disaster occurred. Shortly after that, Express Van Haulage of Dundee received calls from two of their drivers who had also seen the crash. Jake Young of Finlarig Terrace was driving south. 'It was like Hiroshima… it threw up half of the road away in front of us… I pulled up and there was this huge fireball going over the houses,' he said. Some Dundee families had relatives in Lockerbie and one man's son lived just 150 yards from the main crash site.

Two days later, a team of four specialist-trained social workers went to Lockerbie to help American relatives who were arriving and shocked local people and relatives of victims. A second team was sent some days later. Some of these social workers from Dundee had been involved in the aftermath of the Piper Alpha tragedy and had received special training for civil disaster work which involves very extensive grief counselling. Three of the original team worked nonstop at the scene for six days over the Christmas period in what was then the world's worst terrorist incident.

In 1984 the world first heard about Sandy Kydd's gyroscopic anti-gravity machine. Kydd, a Shell engineer, built the prototype in his garden shed. In 1988 Grampian TV produced a documentary about it. 'The machine's possibilities are enormous' said Dr Bill Ferrier, senior physicist at Dundee University. Professor Eric Laithwaite of Imperial College London, who had pioneered the high-speed linear train, described it as 'a potential space device devised by an ingenious engineer'. Grampian reporter Ron Thompson wrote a book on the subject, *Beyond 2001*, published in 1990. Meanwhile, a 'white knight' investor, Australian millionaire Noel Carroll, funded the Kydd family's move to Melbourne. The device was tested in California and Colorado and development work continues to create practical applications for the device.

AIDS and Pressure on the Social Services

In the late 1980s the spectre of HIV arrived and Dundee soon shared with Edinburgh the unenviable title of AIDS capital of Europe. In April 1986 it was revealed that all the AIDS carriers in Dundee were intravenous drug users who had contracted the disease by sharing needles. It was estimated that HIV had arrived in Dundee 12 to 18 months previously. There was no case of full-blown AIDS in Tayside in 1986 although 62 adults were carriers of the virus, including three children, and all had been detected after presenting with minor infections. Although the Edinburgh problem was twice the size of Tayside's, the estimated local cost of the disease was £10 million, which put it on the scale of cholera epidemics of the past. There was no local clinic and those with the disease had to attend the genito-urinary department at the DRI until the new HIV unit was established at King's Cross Hospital. As the full horror of the infection began to be apparent new health education campaigns and special outreach teams were set up.

The NHS in Dundee was making great strides in other areas. In the early 1980s, Tayside's first test-tube baby was born at Ninewells and organ transplantation increased so that it became a routine procedure. Despite the trauma of the Thatcher NHS reforms late in the decade, health service provision expanded. In 1988 an influential study was published by the cardiovascular epidemiology unit at Ninewells, which showed that Scotland's heart disease rate was the worst in Europe, and smoking rates were very high. Dundee medical staff were at the forefront of the mid-1980s responses to improve diet and health which included the foundation of the Scottish heart and arterial disease risk prevention unit.

CHAPTER 6

The Discovery of Optimism

High-Tech Leads The Way

Dundee began the 1990s with an accolade as Scotland's 'Recycling City' for its efforts to collect paper, glass and metal. Traditional sectors enjoyed a slight comeback in January 1991, when Dundee Textiles built a finishing plant at Riverside and two vast 90,000-ton Venezuelan tankers, the *Sanchio Phoenix* and the *Handy Sonata*, brought crude oil to Brigg's Camperdown refinery. They were able to dock because of £1 million upgrading work and the arrival of a large Mannesman Demag mobile crane to handle larger cargoes. A remote radar surveillance system which gives the port control a picture of all vessel movement in the Tay estuary was only the second of its kind in Europe. The Dundee port was privatised in 1995 under the guidelines of the Ports Act 1991 and was bought by Forth Ports Plc. Many older-established industrial companies, like Michelin at Baldovie, the sole UK manufacturing facility of car tyres, remain of course and D.C. Thomson, the only Scottish-owned newspaper empire continues to thrive in the city. On 30 March 1992, the *Courier* printed news on its front page, changing the traditions of 175 years, and co-ordinated the change with the use of colour. The company, which remains one of Dundee's largest employers, built a massive new headquarters at Kingsway East and moved many of their operations there in stages in the early 1990s.

One of the biggest commercial stories of the 1980s was William Low. The grocery company had begun in 1868 in Ure Street and by 1936 had 85 branches, having swallowed up many of the smaller local chains including some Johnston Stores. Their explosive performance in the late 1980s and early 1990s foundered in the recession with competition from cut-price stores, although in 1991 they opened a superstore at Camperdown leisure park and in 1993 a large head office at Baird Avenue with 320 employees. In July 1994 William Low's 57 stores were subjected to a 'friendly' takeover by Tesco.

Having previously had only 16 outlets in Scotland, Tesco was now Scotland's largest supermarket, and promised to ensure the jobs of existing employees and of local suppliers, but many were sad to see the demise of a genuine Dundee-based retail empire.

Tesco stores were unusually busy on 19 November 1994 when thousands of Dundonians queued at the new terminals of the National Lottery there and in other stores and post offices to buy tickets for the first-ever draw. Since then, three Dundonians have come up with five numbers plus bonus ball wins, the most recent, in 1998, winning £165,000.

> 1996 was the 80th birthday year of Dr Pat McPherson, life president of Wright Dental Group and one of Dundee's most remarkable post-war industrialists. Educated at Dundee High School, he joined F.H. Wright dental manufacturers in Dundee after World War Two and became chief executive and then chairman, during which time it became Britain's largest dental company with subsidiary companies all over the world, a leading exporter of false teeth and dental instruments. In 1986 he received the honorary degree of Doctor of Laws from Dundee University and in 1988 an OBE. He was instrumental in bringing Professor Roland Wolf to Dundee's biomedical centre.

The Dundee Business Support Group was formed in 1991 with representatives from nine private sector companies including NCR, whose 150,000sq ft research and design facility at Wester Gourdie is a new project second in size only to the Scottish Parliament building at Holyrood. There had been bad as well as good news in the traditional industries: APW closed their Riverside Avenue factory with the loss of 200 jobs, TDI Batteries halved its workforce of 190, Madison Cables axed 70, almost all of its Dundee payroll, Trak Microwave, which had sent its microwave components en-route to Saturn via NASA missions, paid off 56, and Levis closed entirely in 2002 with the loss of 462 jobs, ending a 30-year association with Dundee which had seen it employ 600 at its peak in 1995. (See *Appendix, Figure 4*)

Dundee had developed in the biotech sector with 1,600 employees, and by the end of the millenium, call centres were employing nearly 2,000. Any bad news was being drowned by the flood of stories involving new high-tech, biomedical and medical research advances and new electronics company start-ups. Out at Invergowrie the Scottish Crop Research Institute remains a major international research centre. Many of the new companies are at the cutting edge of technology. Highly innovative research is conducted by Shield Diagnostics and AMCET, another advanced materials research 'spin out' company. Cyclacel – formed by Sir David Lane in 1996 to develop products for cancer therapy – and Axis-Shield, producing *in vitro* diagnostic kits, have over 70 products at present. Upstate Discovery work in the cell signalling product field and Alchemy was formed to explore rapid test diagnostic technology. Dundee also has excellence in the medical research field with Professor Albert Cuschieri's world-class innovations in 'keyhole' surgery, and the largest life sciences and research community in the UK outside Oxford or Cambridge. Another growth area is electronics and virtual reality technology. Abertay University has played a key role in some of these developments, promoting spin-out companies such as VIS Entertainment, Visual Sciences, Denki and Real Time World in the virtual reality entertainment sector. This led to the Scottish Computer Games Alliance moving its headquarters from Glasgow to Dundee. Dundee's biomedical core is expanding exponentially with many collaborative projects between Ninewells and Dundee University, which has developed expertise in intellectual property management. Its Centre for Enterprise Management has over 80 live patents on its books.

At BT's call centre at Technology Park, the picture shows Tom Sheridan, chief executive of Barclays stockbrokers. (Alan Richardson photography)

City of Discovery! Professor Sir David Lane in the Wellcome Trust Biocentre, Dundee University. (Alan Richardson photography)

Professor Sir David Lane with staff in a laboratory, Wellcome Trust Biocentre. (Alan Richardson photography)

The Wellcome Trust
Biocentre in Hawkhill, a
£13 million 'Citadel of
Science' with the older
Medical Sciences
Institute in the
background. (A.M.
Scott)

Abertay University's £8
million library won
several design awards. It
was opened by the
Queen on 30 June 1998
and is the start of large-
scale development of the
Bell Street area to form
a new campus as student
numbers increase. (A.M.
Scott)

Left: Dudhope Castle, the ancestral 16th-century home of the Constables of Dundee and later of Graham of Claverhouse, in its new guise as the home of Dundee Business School, a collaboration between Abertay University and the Chamber of Commerce. (A.M. Scott)

Right: New building at the Medipark, Ninewells, with the hospital in the background. (A.M. Scott)

The western extension of Ninewells incorporates the accident and emergency department since the closure of the DRI in 1998. (A.M. Scott)

Octocentenary

The major event in Dundee's civic calendar in 1991 was the Octocentenary. Dundee's 800 years as a Royal Burgh provided a worthy excuse for a year-long celebration. In March 1990, brash, cowboy hat-wearing Montreal-born Henny King arrived in Dundee. The celebrations got under way with a magnificent Hogmanay party in City Square, filmed by Grampian and Sky TV, featuring acrobats, fire-eaters, street performers and jugglers. Bands played, bells were

rung from the churches, and a monster 800 'sweet' was smashed for distribution to local children. St Mary's was floodlit, a light show probed the heavens above the Law and there were fireworks displays. Attendance topped 70,000 with a crowd of 25,000 partying in City Square to see in the New Year. There were almost no incidents although some youths smashed bottles and some buses were vandalised. There was an acute shortage of toilets and the City Square on the morning after, in driving rain and strong winds, looked like a bombsite. The *Sunday Times* poured faint praise; 'Hogmanay to the rescue of Dundee bash' and, after referring to the 'public confusion, disinterest and hostility focussed on Henny King asked "Can the city afford to keep it up?"'

There had been some disquiet when it was revealed that within a month of her arrival, Henny King had been promoted to director level and her salary raised by £5,000. Many were critical of the sexism of the Wild West cowgirl troupe clad in tasselled mini-skirts, stetsons and high boots – the Cactus Prairies – who chanted a cheerleader type chant written by King. Plans to create the world's biggest ever clootie dumpling were dashed when experts opined it would reach 'critical mass' during cooking and explode. The concept of a McGonagall-type 'worst poetry' competition was shelved after criticism of the negative image this would create and the fact that right-wing critic Auberon Waugh was to be the judge. There was a furore when it was revealed that the festival launch was to be in Glasgow. Under sustained criticism and with a low level of donations from local businesses, Labour leader Ian Luke felt it necessary to declare that the programme 'was always going to be a council-led programme.' One of the events which went ahead was the draping of a gasometer at East Dock Street to make it look like a cake, with temporary electric candles on the top. But these, being only 60 watts, were in the event barely visible. It was also difficult to gauge the success of the event on 11

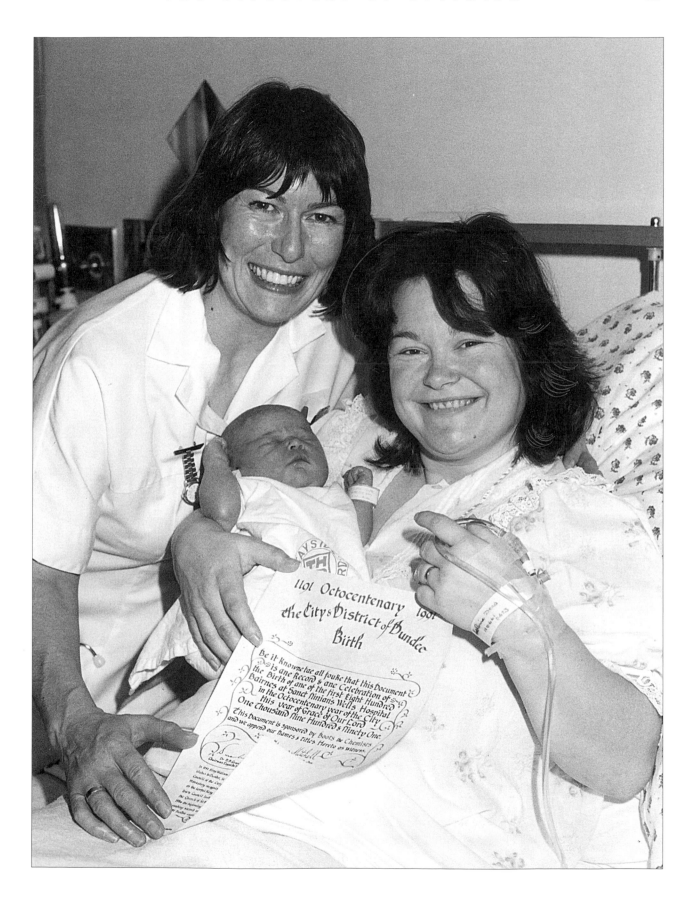

September when at 11 minutes past 11am, everyone in the city was to open their window and sing the *Bonnets O' Bonnie Dundee*. The *Courier* had printed the words and local radio stations had played the song several times to give everyone a chance for a rehearsal. But as the year wore on, the festival lost momentum and critics like Conservative Councillor Neil Powrie were scathing about Labour councillors dressing up in medieval costumes 'just to get their names in the paper.'

The street carnival on 1 June had the blessing of good weather and some 20,000 flocked to the city centre to see the history floats and exotic Chinese dragons, acrobats piloting steel Rhonrad wheels along the High Street and the fireworks display. An estimated 50,000 attended events during the 15 hours of the festivities. RAF jets flew overhead, bands played, actors re-enacted scenes from Dundee's history, Jacobites brawled at the Old Steeple and Ron Coburn acted as Dundee's Bellman. 'I feel the whole day was an absolute success,' said Henny King, 'and the wonderful reaction of the crowds just shows that.' It was, according to the *Courier*, the biggest organised celebration in the city's history. Delegations from twin cities Orléans, Alexandria, Wurzburg and Zadar had been present. The community drama *Bridge* was performed in Meadowside on 4–6 July around a specially constructed prop bridge. Another eye-catching event featured 800 over-60s wearing the 800 logo teeshirt doing their exercise routines in the Caird Hall under the watchful eye of Dorothy Dobson. The city featured on TV-AM on 13 September in a feature introduced

Henny King at the Octocentenary Grand Parade, 1 June 1991. (The Sunday Post, Dundee)

Dundee 800th birthday parade, High Street. (The Courier, Dundee)

Previous page: Dundee Day; view of Reform Street crowds and Dundee High School. (The Courier, Dundee)

The scene in Albert Square as the cast of Bridge *rehearse, July 1991.* (The Courier, Dundee)

by Ulrika Johnsson. The year-long programme culminated in a second Hogmanay party in the city centre which was, inevitably, more muted than the previous year.

It was inevitable that a festival of this scale should find it difficult to sustain interest throughout an entire year. The Tourist Board reported a 5,000 rise in inquiries during the year and Ian Luke predicted 'we are now about to reap the benefits of the international exposure our celebrations achieved.' The total bill, some £300,000, was, he declared, excellent value for money. Lord Provost Mitchell commented: 'Henny King is full of enthusiasm and people like that do make mistakes. But she put her heart and soul into the job.' Few could disagree with that. After the tragic death of her husband, artist Edmund Caswell, Henny chose to make her home in her adopted city.

Living in a Campus City

In 1990 statistics were released which showed that a Dundee University graduate was eight times more likely to get immediate employment than a graduate of any other UK university. Perhaps this was not altogether a surprise, given that the chancellor of the university was Sir James Whyte Black, a Nobel Prize winner in 1988 for discovering beta blockers. The 'father of analytical pharmacology' was voted the 'Scotsman of the Decade' in 1980. In less than

four decades, Dundee University had become a powerhouse of teaching and research, with an annual turnover of £110 million and a research income of £30.6 million. It had attracted an annual roll of 12,000 students, with 1,600

The Catherine Wheel in the Octocentenary Carnival, 30 December 1991. (The Courier, Dundee)

teaching and research staff, and it is the city's fourth largest employer. In the *Guardian*'s UK Subject Assessment report it was the top Scottish university and the sixth in the UK for graduate employment, with 98 percent of graduates in employment or training within six months. Its department of English was rated top in the UK and its faculties of art and design, biosciences, anatomy and physiology and pharmacology were all in the top five.

The university is unquestionably one of the biggest contributors to the life and wellbeing of Dundee, a long way

Perth Road and Dundee University Tower. (A.M. Scott)

Dundee University's new library and plaza. With 39,000 students (including all categories), Dundee has an active and youthful social life. (A.M. Scott)

from the modest hopes of Principal Wimberley in 1947. One tenth of the population of Dundee are students – some 39,000 including all part-timers and all categories. Collaborations between the two universities and especially the Duncan of Jordanstone art faculty, which is rated top in Scotland for its fine art, design, TV and imaging and architecture courses, has led to the Visual Research Centre in DCA and other joint projects, as well as co-operation with St Andrews University. Dundee University has expanded to include the huge Gardyne Road site as its new faculty of education. Not to be outdone, Abertay University, whose £8 million library in Bell Street won plaudits of its own, plans a new £4 million piazza and student centre. Work is to start in 2002 at Dundee Rep for a new Scottish Dance Theatre, to complement the Scottish School of Contemporary Dance at the Space, at the Kingsway campus of Dundee College, which, completed in October 2001 costing £5 million, had allowed Dundee to claim the title 'City of Dance'. Dundee Rep hosts the only full-time company of actors in Scotland.

However, in the 1990s there was also a city-wide contraction of schools, cut-backs and some closures. Linlathen was closed because of a falling roll and demolished and sold for development. Parents were concerned about the proposed merger of Rockwell and Kirkton High School. The BBC's *Frontline* programme on 22 March 1996 featured scenes at a parents' meeting where Kirkton was described as 'the Bronx'. Kirkton residents resented the slur but the Rockwell School board decided to consider opting-out of local authority

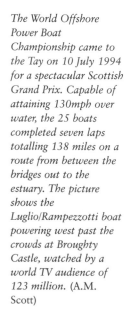

The World Offshore Power Boat Championship came to the Tay on 10 July 1994 for a spectacular Scottish Grand Prix. Capable of attaining 130mph over water, the 25 boats completed seven laps totalling 138 miles on a route from between the bridges out to the estuary. The picture shows the Luglio/Rampezzotti boat powering west past the crowds at Broughty Castle, watched by a world TV audience of 123 million. (A.M. Scott)

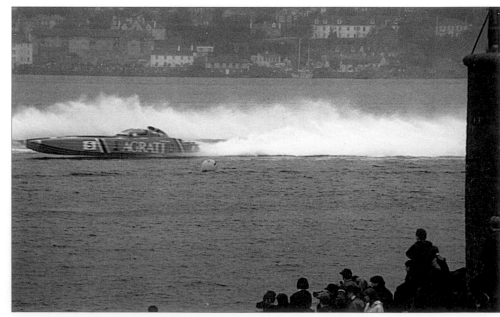

control, even though the staff and teaching unions were opposed to the idea. Other local schools became involved in the mergers and cutbacks debate. The £9 million DCA, completed in 1999, won architecture accolades with its galleries, two cinema screens and state-of-the-art printmaking workshops, and was immediately popular with the public. It is the centrepiece of a new cultural strategy which encompasses other cultural initiatives such as the ongoing Dundee Book Prize. The buzz about a 'cultural quarter' shows that the city has started to turn around its 'disenchanting at close quarters' image. The *Lonely Planet Guide 2001*, not known for its willingness to lavish praise, commented: 'Now the dour, desolate

Dundee Contemporary Arts, Nethergate, has proved very popular since it opened in 1999 and is a cornerstone of the city's new 'cultural quarter'. (A.M. Scott)

Dundee of legend is fading. The city has cultural vigour and ambition. Its real asset is its people, among the friendliest, most welcoming and most entertaining people you'll meet.'

Fond farewells

The Gulf War erupted in 1991 and filled TV screens with frightening images of technological warfare as the Allies countered the Iraqi Guard's invasion of Kuwait. The high-profile war heightened fears about the numerous local service personnel sent to the region. The *Sunday Post* set up a seven days a week helpline for relatives of serving personnel to try to allay fears and to act as an avenue of communication between the forces and the public. One Dundee soldier, Staff Sergeant Steve Robertson, a 33-year-old former pupil of Craigie High School, was later awarded the British Empire Medal. As a cartographic draughtsman with the Royal Engineers, he had been in the thick of the fighting, mapping the front-line positions. 'I'm pleased to have been awarded the BEM' he said after the ceremony. 'It isn't something you expect, when you're just doing your job.'

In July 1991, the 350 volunteers of the Royal Observer Corps, No.28 Group ROC Base, Craigiebarns, were stood down on its 50th anniversary and the familiar black berets and armbands with the legend 'forewarned is forearmed' were put away in drawers.

Dundonians turned out to commemorate the D-Day landings with a 50th anniversary parade involving veterans and detachments from the services. The parade, on 4 June 1994, snaked through the city centre from Dundee High

The modern design of the Sensation Science Centre, built on the south side of the DCA, has attracted comment since it opened in June 2000. (A.M. Scott)

Tom McDonald died on 22 June 1995 at the untimely age of 43. He represented Lochee West for more than 20 years and had served as Lord Provost since May 1992. (The Courier, Dundee)

School to the Garden of Remembrance, where wreaths were laid and small crosses placed to commemorate Dundee's fallen. Lord Provost Tom McDonald took the salute at the march past and a bugler from the Sea Cadets played the last post after a piper played a lament. Twelve veterans from Dundee aptly described in the *Courier* as the 'Doughty Dozen' returned to Normandy, where they had taken part in the landings in June 1944. Fred Potter of Dundee Royal Naval Association laid a wreath at the grave of Dundee Black Watch Piper George Bruce at Bayeux. Another of the dozen, former Lieutenant-Colonel Edward Traynor, president of the City of Dundee British Legion, recalled serving with the Parachute Regiment in the battle for 'Pegasus Bridge'. On 6 May 1995, the Royal Naval Association held a commemorative VE day dance at the RNA Club in St Roques Lane, which some veterans attended in wartime uniforms.

On 12 March 1994, Dundee's Caird Hall hosted the Labour Party's Scottish Conference, addressed by their new British leader, John Smith. Exactly two months later, Mr Smith was dead. 'The Nation Unites In Mourning' ran the *Courier* headline on 12 May, declaring that 'grief crossed the political divide'. Mr Smith was later to be described as 'one of the greatest Prime Ministers Britain never had'. Dundonians queued to sign the condolence book in the City Chambers.

On 22 June 1995 Dundee's Lord Provost Tom McDonald died following a seven-hour operation at Ninewells. Although only 43, he had represented Lochee West for more than 20 years. Tributes poured in for a man held in high regard across the political spectrum. His funeral on the 24th was attended by hundreds and hundreds more watched the cortège from the Thanksgiving Mass at St Andrews Cathedral to Balgay Cemetery. The steeple bells rang half-muffled as they had for John Smith. The eulogy was read by Labour council leader Kate McLean, who said: 'He cared passionately about Dundee, abhorred injustice in all its forms and believed that individuals could and should make a difference.'

On 27 June 1995 the royal yacht *Britannia* berthed in strong sunshine at the Princess Alexandra Wharf as Prince Charles made a solo two-day visit to the area to see the Lily Walker Centre for the Homeless, Verdant Works and to stroll in City Square. But the sudden death of Diana, Princess of Wales, on 1 September 1997 shocked the world and led to many Dundonians recalling the two official visits she had made to Dundee with Charles. On 8 September 1983 she had toured Keiller's Confectionery in Mains Loan and held a walkabout at the factory gates so that the itinerary overran by 20 minutes. Then, three years later, she had visited Roxburghe House, the Royal Victoria Hospital and the Dr Barnardo's family support centre in Dudhope Street. She was a popular figure in Dundee and ex-Lord Provost James Gowans, recalling the visits, revealed that she was his 'favourite royal.' The *Courier* produced a comprehensive supplement 'Diana: A Life In Pictures' and a condolence book was opened in City Chambers. The tragedy halted campaigning in the Devolution Referendum and many businesses closed as a mark of respect. On Saturday 6 September, the city centre came to a standstill as the funeral was taking place at Westminster Abbey. Lord Provost Mervyn Rolfe conducted a two-minute silence on the steps of the Caird Hall, where well-wishers had left bunches of flowers and a lone piper played a lament to the 'Queen of the Peoples' Hearts'. Local music shops geared themselves for huge sales of Elton John's new version of *Candle In The Wind* and hundreds queued to sign the condolence book in the entrance hallway of City Chambers, which took on the atmosphere of a shrine with a single candle and a photograph of Diana. The opening hours had to be extended and a second, third and fourth book had to be provided to cope with the demand. The Dundee Flower Show, held that weekend, which was the biggest-ever since it began in 1988, closed on Saturday morning and re-opened in the afternoon. The attendance did not, for obvious reasons, quite match the previous year's all-time record.

Trials and Tribulations

The saga of the city's Labour Clubs was in the headlines in April 1991 with the long-delayed trial of the former manager of the Whitfield Club, James Martin, at Dundee Sheriff Court. Martin, a former councillor, was charged with embezzling nearly £10,000 from the club in 1985. Prior to the trial, he had collaborated with the Channel 4 documentary *In The Red*, which made allegations against senior Labour activists. Days before the trial began he received a Mafia-style death threat in the form of two 'with sympathy' cards containing .22 bullets and the single word *Omerta* (Italian for conspiracy of silence) sent to his home and place of work. Police conducted forensic tests on the Dundee-postmarked envelopes. During the trial, sensational allegations were made that the club had been, in the words of the prosecution, 'systematically looted for the benefit of Labour Party members.' An estimated £100,000 was missing from the four clubs. The police report in 24 volumes had taken 3,500 man-hours to prepare at a cost to the taxpayer of £36,000. One of Martin's allegations was that George Galloway and Councillors Rennie and Christie, having run out of money while attending Labour Conference in Blackpool, had instructed Jack Stewart to travel to Dundee and bring Martin down with the Whitfield Club chequebook in order to write a cheque to fund their entertainment. It was alleged that certain Labour councillors had availed themselves of free drinks at the clubs and been able to get handouts for political activities from the till.

Martin's plea of not guilty to most of the charges was accepted at the start of the trial and he pleaded guilty to the less serious charge of a £5,000 loan fraud and was sentenced to 150 hours community service and ordered to repay £2,000 to the bank. The trial, expected to last three weeks, was over in less than a day. There was public disquiet that in the wake of such serious allegations the police had so little to show for their efforts.

Labour were to have further problems in the 1990s with the 'Borthwick Affair', when their former leader on Tayside Regional Council became an Independent and successfully held off Labour challenges at successive elections in the Downfield St Mary's area. A Labour regional councillor was fined for fraud in November 1994 and a second, Roads and Transport Convenor Raymond Mennie, was convicted in February 1993, with Conservative Robert Pullar, of corruptly soliciting money from a roadside development application on the Dundee to Perth A85 and received a one-year jail sentence.

In June 1994 the SNP's Alan MacCartney took the North-East Scotland seat in the European elections, but five weeks previously in the regional elections Labour won 16 Dundee seats to the SNP's one. This, the Whitfield division, had been secured on the narrowest of possible margins, a single disputed ballot paper decided after three recounts. The SNP's Jim Duthie, who had previously won the seat in a by-election, had to endure the legal examination of the ballot paper when his Labour challenger George Barr subsequently obtained permission from the Sheriff Principal of Perth Sheriff Court on the grounds that it had two marks on it and should be considered as a spoilt vote. The paper had a cross against Duthie's name and a scribbled circle in the box for the Lib Dem candidate. It was decided that the vote showed clear intention and should stand.

There were some bitter local issues, none more so than on 14 April 1995, when the St Mary's Action Group, assisted by Councillor Borthwick, began its campaign against the siting of the Vulnerable Families Project at St Mary's. The aftermath of 22 October 1991, when two of Broughty Ferry's farm-style rail crossing gates were wrecked by a speeding train, led to a prolonged dispute since Scotrail insisted on using modern, remote-controlled gates. The community council won the day but Scotrail, who modernised the station (at which few trains stop during the daytime), removed the listed station building allegedly for repairs. Other local flashpoints included the council budget cuts which threatened the removal of 16 flower beds at a popular esplanade park. On 9 September 1997, the Friends of Barnhill Rock Garden was established by residents volunteering to help the council maintain the park.

In September 1997, Scotland witnessed campaigning in the Devolution Referendum. Labour, SNP, the Liberal Democrats and trade unionists put aside their differences to collaborate in the 'Yes Yes' campaign and formed a local committee of 'Scotland Forward'. There was little local activity from the 'Scotland Says No' campaign. Voting in the 131 Dundee polling stations on 9

September was brisk from 7am to 10pm despite early fears about apathy and cheers rang out in the Caird Hall in the early hours of the 10th when the turnout was finalised at 55.7 percent. Of 65,211 Dundonians who voted, 76 percent voted for a Parliament, and only slightly less, 65.5 percent, for 'tax varying powers'. Loud choruses of *Flower of Scotland* erupted on a rare occasion of cross-party jubilation – which was to evaporate when the parties fought the elections to the new Scottish Parliament which were held on 6 May 1999. Labour formed a minority administration with the assistance of the Lib Dems under the leadership of Donald Dewar.

The Timex Dispute

One of the most traumatic and divisive political events in Dundee's recent history was the Timex dispute of January to March 1993. The company was one of the first to move in to the local industrial scene in the late 1940s, a core employer at its Camperdown factory on Harrison Road. The dispute began on 30 January 1993 after 60 hours of talks between the AEEU and management failed to resolve the question of rotational lay-offs among the 300 hourly-paid employees. Gordon Samson, the union district secretary, and Harry McLevy, the Scottish regional officer, made a last-ditch attempt to change the mind of Managing Director Peter Hall. The strike was widely reported on television and became increasingly bitter when Timex Director Fred Olson arrived and began bussing in hired workers, denounced at the gates by the pickets as 'scab labour'. Members of the MSF union were still working and management and full-time staff attempted to keep production going, but this proved impossible. The company sought, and failed to obtain, an interim interdict at the Sheriff Court to prevent pickets from stopping vehicles and pedestrians entering the factory.

The police presence was stepped up as the exchanges at the gates became increasingly hostile. The company attempted to obtain an interim interdict at the Court of Session in Edinburgh to prevent the two full-time and two local AEEU officials from organising or inciting employees at the gates. This was granted against John Kydd senior, John Kydd junior, William Leslie and Charlie Malone, who were effectively running the action. The company tried to extend the interdict to all 320 named employees – and this was refused. The strike became a cause célèbre and received considerable support from the Labour movement in Scotland and England. The local MPs pleaded for talks to be resumed at a mass meeting of the workers in the Caird Hall. On 12 February a six-hour meeting broke up with the unions claiming Peter Hall had added new conditions which could not be met by the workforce. At a further mass meeting on 18 February, the workforce overwhelmingly rejected Timex's final offer, a four-point plan which included a pay freeze, a cut in fringe benefits and little movement on rotational lay-offs. The company retaliated by issuing termination notices to all the employees (including the 17 who had

'Scaaab!' A familiar scene at the gates of the Timex factory in Harrison Road during the divisive and highly publicised dispute from January to March 1993. (The Courier, Dundee)

continued to work) and the action became a lock-out. There was considerable criticism of the way Peter Hall handled the dispute and his airy declaration that he would recruit new employees immediately – he had hundred of applications in hand – and that he wanted to boost numbers to 700 because 'prospects were good' rubbed salt into the wounds. As it turned out, Timex never re-opened.

James McIntosh Patrick at his studio in Magdalen Yard Road with a print of his painting 'A Country Lane, Perthshire' on 20 December 1994. One of Scotland's greatest 20th-century landscape painters, he was born in Dundee in 1907 and died in the city in 1998. Citizen of the Year in 1979, he was awarded an OBE in 1997 and various honorary doctorates. (Evening Telegraph, Dundee)

Melissa McCreadie offers a posy to the Queen on 3 July 1991 in the High Street. (Evening Telegraph, Dundee)

The Queen with Lord Provost Thomas Mitchell on 3 July 1991, after her visit to open Expo 800, a four-day showcase of more than 150 Tayside companies held in a tented 4,000sq ft exhibition space at Riverside. (Evening Telegraph, Dundee)

Crime Headlines

In the early 1990s, Dundee police were dealing with 150 gang-related incidents a week, the most serious problem they faced, but major incidents were rare and most categories of crime were on the decrease. The introduction of CCTV into the city centre in April 1996 reduced crime by 27 percent in the first six months. One incident that made the headlines over the New Year period in 1990 was the disappearance of 25-year-old handicapped man Nealle Wilson from Ardler. A friendly, cheerful young man with many friends, he had a mental age of 10 and was an epileptic. He disappeared without trace after attending a New Year party in Menzieshill. When his body was recovered from the Sidlaws near Scotston Farm on 11 February 1993, his family were convinced that he had been murdered since he was unable to travel far on his own, having club feet. Nevertheless, a fatal accident inquiry was unable to conclude that a crime had been committed.

On 23 February 1993 an armed gang raided the GPO in Ward Road. Two hooded men made off with a five-figure sum after threatening staff with sawn-off shotguns. They made their getaway in a wine-coloured Vauxhall Cavalier up Constitution Road. The raid occurred just minutes after security men had delivered the money to the Post Office from Littlewoods. Police suspected that four men had been involved.

Members of Dundee's Muslim community gather for a ceremony to bless the site of the new mosque in Miln Street on 14 November 1997. (The Courier, Dundee)

Armed incidents are rare in Dundee, not so in America. Andrew De Vries, a Dundee oilman, was shot dead in Houston on 7 January 1994 by local businessman Jeffrey Agee, who mistook him for a burglar. His wife Alison, who lived in Aberdeen, and his mother, of Albany Drive, West Ferry, were shocked to hear of what the Houston police called 'an unusual and tragic situation'. An Aberdonian colleague, Sydney Graves, recounted events after they had attended a country and western bar. De Vries had rung the front doorbell of a house in a Houston suburb at 4am and then knocked at the back door. Agee fired three shots through the glass door. Texan law permitted the use of 'deadly force' for protection if a person felt himself or his property to be under threat. The incident made world news and a TV crew from Houston arrived in Dundee to test local reaction on 5 February, the day after a Grand Jury had decided 8–4 not to press charges against Agee. A female juror was angry enough to make a public comment: 'There was no warning,' she said, 'no nothing. He just fired.'

For weeks, in early 1993, Dundee was gripped by what came to be known as 'the headless corpse murder' after a decapitated body was found on the Law by two young dogwalkers. Forensic examination of the gruesome find took some time but the identity of the victim was established as 52-year-old Gordon Dunbar, who lived in a guesthouse on Victoria Road. The police soon established that his murderer was 43-year-old Alastair Thompson, who had enticed the victim into his flat in Butterburn Court in December 1992, dismembered the body and disposed of the parts. Although the head was never found, Thomson, described as a dangerous psychopath, was jailed for life on 22 January 1994 with a recommendation that he serve a minimum of 20 years for what the judge described as 'this nauseating and barbaric murder'. Thompson immediately lodged an appeal but this was dismissed.

The tragedy of the massacre of innocent school children and their teacher at Dunblane Primary School in March 1996 by Thomas Hamilton reverberated around the world. A condolence book was opened in the City Chambers to allow Dundee people to express their deepest sympathies to the families of the dead children and their teacher. After the event, more than 20 weapons were handed in to Tayside police by sickened gun-owners even before the government announced a gun amnesty. Tayside had one of the highest rates of ownership of weapons per head of the population in Scotland, more than 24,000 legally-held weapons. Many Dundee schools organised ceremonies of respect and held one-minute silences.

The senseless murder of a civil servant, Anne Nicoll of Byron Street, while out walking her dog in the wooded area on the lower slopes of the Law on 2 August 2001 outraged public opinion, but the crime was dwarfed by the scale of the tragedy which engulfed the world a month later. A young Broughty Ferry man was killed in what was the most horrific event of the century so far. Derek Sword, a 29-year-old former pupil of Monifieth High School and BA Hons graduate of Dundee Institute of Technology was employed as an investment banker with Keefe Bruyette Woods in Manhattan. He was at work on the 89th floor of the south tower of the World Trade Centre early on 11 September 2001 when the plane hijacked by terrorists hit the north tower. He immediately telephoned his mother and father to tell them he was alright. He made a second call minutes later when the second hijacked jet crashed into the south tower, and told his parents he was fleeing the burning building, but nothing was heard of him again. Derek was a champion squash player, a former Scottish junior international and champion of the New York Athletics Club and his parents inaugurated World Squash Day, a professional tournament, in his honour in London, four months after the tragedy.

Beyond The Millenium

As Dundee moves into a new millenium there are many significant problems. The population continues to decline with some projections suggesting it will drop to 137,259 by summer 2011 (see *Appendix, Figure 2*). The road bridge, in its fifth decade, clearly needs to be replaced. The Joseph Rowntree Foundation study *The Geography of Poverty and Wealth*, published in 1994, had found Dundee to be an area of 'concentrated poverty'. The study, based on indices of car ownership, unemployment, housing and supplementary benefit between 1981–1991, cannot be glossed over. (See *Appendix, Figures 3, 7, 8 and 9*) The city faces the cost of widening major routes in the area and guaranteeing the financial security of even key STB five-star rated tourist attractions such as Discovery and Verdant Mill, which seem on occasion insecure. Much of the city's cultural life is dependent on central funding and there has been a long-term failure to attract significant numbers of tourists, except day visitors.

Tay Bridge station is the only one of four Dundee railway stations to survive into the 21st century. The council's official Daimler, TS1, parked on the right of the picture, indicates that the Lord Provost is in the vicinity on official business. (A.M. Scott)

Dundee is still a city in flux, hamstrung by overtly narrow boundaries. The peripheral expansion of housing and development is disconnected from the central core, which contains many areas in need of renewal. With the Scottish Parliament now in place, hopes are high that a significant shift of civil service personnel may come to the city. Some already have. The Pension Service Centre at Claverhouse is one of 20 in the UK, with 550 staff employed to process pensioners' benefits. A new office complex on the waterfront is to be the joint headquarters of the Scottish Commission for the Regulation of Care and the Scottish Social Services Executive, bringing 150 civil servants to Dundee; an early success for the cross-party, multi-organisational Tayside Civil Service Jobs Campaign.

Beyond the 'whalebone arch' gateway to the Wellgate Library, the Hilltown multis in the background and on the left, Dundee College. (A.M. Scott)

Dundee's City Council-owned airport almost shut down after Business Air was swallowed by British Midland, leading to a loss of the Manchester service. For a period, only small planes of Tayside Aviation and occasional holiday flights to Jersey used the airport. Then Scot Airways (formerly Suckling) arrived. In 1997 Neil Kinnock, EU Transport Commissioner, opened a £1 million terminal and since then 100,000 passengers have used the service to London, but there is a need to expand to fly new routes, including flights to a major international hub. A Dundonian, Brian Souter, the founder of Stagecoach, was the 'white knight' who put up £1 million to underwrite Suckling, which led to success.

Passenger numbers have increased to 1,100 a week, including 250 on one day in 2001.

Dundee In Partnership 2001–2006 is the plan for the future, a 'wish list' which sets out a vision for a vibrant and attractive city, offering real choice and opportunity in a strong and sustainable city economy. The six themes of economy and enterprise, social inclusion, lifelong learning, health and care, sustainability and community safety set out progress indicators which include stabilising the population decline and increasing employment from 79,500 in February 2001 by 1 percent per year to 83,500 by 2006.

Major priorities include tackling the 7.2 percent unemployment rate and the 33.2 percent of households receiving housing benefits. Statistics show that average Dundee earnings are below the Scottish average, (see *Appendix, Figure 9*). There is a need to reduce chronic smoking rates among 12–15s from 14 percent, and tackle the associated high rate of coronary and cancer deaths and the pregnancy rate of the 13–15s.

However, there are many positive signs. The restoration of Gardyne's Land in the High Street for use as a tourist hostel seems to show a new sensitivity about heritage. The Summer Festival is a cornucopia of lively events which could act as a focus for increased tourist revenue. The new £50 million City Quay development is a major step forward and will include a 150-bedroom four-star hotel with conference facilities and 245 flats and houses with restaurants and bars bringing life back to the riverfront. Dundee has done itself

Demolition of Dundee Royal Infirmary continuing in January 2000. Some of the structure, which dates from 1855, will be retained for conversion to private flats. (The Courier, Dundee)

The Mexican Navy vessel Cuauhtemoc, *which visited Dundee in August 2001. One of nine tall ships which honoured RRS* Discovery *in her centenary year after the Cutty Sark Tall Ships race in Esberg, Denmark, she fired a 21-gun salute before berthing alongside the* Shabab Oman *(formerly the* Captain Scott, *now owned by the Sultan of Oman) in the Camperdown dock. (The Courier, Dundee)*

proud with the establishing of Maggie's Centre at Ninewells – named after Maggie Keswick Jencks – which aims to complement medical treatment, with the ambience of a comfortable home and an attitude which refuses to let fear of death interfere with the business of living. In March 2002 the

Dundee FC's Claudio Caniggia in action at Dens before he was transferred to Rangers. (Alan Richardson photography)

Dark Blues boss Ivano Bonetti and his older brother Dario have brought many exciting players, such as Claudio Caniggia, to Dens from Italy, Argentina, Spain, Georgia and China, in what has become known as Dundee's 'Foreign Legion'. (Alan Richardson photography)

Derek Lilley scores with two minutes to spare against St Johnstone on 12 May 2001 to make it 3-2 at MacDiarmid Park. Dubbed 'the £4 million goal' it kept the Tangerines safe from relegation. At full time, United fans invaded the pitch to celebrate staying up in the Scottish Premier League. (Alan Richardson photography)

John McAllion, Labour MSP for Dundee East, abseiling from Dundee University Tower, one of 150 volunteers who took part in Dundee Abseil Day on 2 September 2000. The MSP made the 100ft descent for the Brittle Bones charity. (Richard McCready)

Shona Robison, Dundee-based SNP MSP on a clean-up of Broughty Beach, with (left) Stewart Hosie and local councillor Ken Guild. (Joe Fitzpatrick)

announcement of a new £15 million grant to build a laboratory research facility, the Centre for Interdisciplinary Research, adjacent to the Wellcome Trust Building, strengthens what is now being referred to as Dundee's 'Citadel of Science' and may employ another 250 biomedical scientists when it is complete. Increasingly there is a perception that it is in Dundee that the battle against cancer, diabetes and other major diseases will be won.

The city is set to launch a bid for a new superstadium to host the Euro 2008 football championships. This will be a joint Dundee FC and Dundee United FC bid for a new 30,000-seater stadium, possibly at Caird Park, which will lead to both clubs closing their existing grounds and sharing the new facility. Dundee Stars ice hockey team entered the British National League in September 2001 with 'the

spirit of the old Dundee Rockets' behind them. The new ice arena at Camperdown is a major sporting venue. Forthill continues to provide a venue for the Scottish national hard court tennis championships.

On the political front, the Labour administration's narrow majority on Dundee City Council was further reduced at the Tay Bridges by-election in 2001, which saw the Liberal Democrats gain their first Dundee councillor since the days of Garnet Wilson. Now Labour's hold on power depends on a single seat over the SNP and pundits predict a very close contest in the next municipal elections in 2003. An embarrassing row over expenses led to the resignation of the first female Lord Provost, Helen Wright, in May 2001. The council have petitioned for the return of Monifieth and Invergowrie to within the city boundaries. As the smallest municipal authority in Scotland, Dundee's services are used by many from outside its boundaries who do not pay for the provision, and the city is, they say, hamstrung by its lack of space and narrow tax base. The reorganisation of Westminster parliamentary constituencies in 2003 may deprive Dundee of one of its MPs or redraw the parliamentary boundaries to include rural areas formerly within the city.

So what is life in Dundee really like now? The city's image is protected by a corps of PR professionals paid to accentuate the positive. Whether there is substance in its various appelations; City of Dance, Campus City, City of Discovery or whether it is still something of a Magnificent Mirage – there is certainly a vibrancy and a self-pride in Dundee, exemplified by the 1996 campaign 'From Dundee and Proud of It' launched by the *Courier* at the same

The 133-year-old Morgan Academy at the height of the blaze on 21 March 2001. (The Courier, Dundee)

A girl ice-skates at
Dundee ice arena at
Camperdown. Opened
on 22 September 2000,
the £7 million venue has
an Olympic-sized ice
pad for skaters and hosts
major ice-hockey
fixtures, with seating for
2,400 fans. (Alan
Richardson
photography)

*The Space at Dundee
College's Kingsway
Campus hosts the
Scottish School of
Contemporary Dance
studios. Completed in
October 2001 at a cost
of £5 million, it is one of
the developments which
allows Dundee to claim
the title of 'City of
Dance'.* (Owen Daily,
Dundee College)

time as a relaunch of the 'City of Discovery' campaign, which has garnered £4 million-worth of publicity, of which 90 percent is positive. In November 1999 the campaign swept the boards at the Scottish Marketing Awards, taking the Grand Prix title as well as the prize for Best Public Sector campaign. The city's relationship with the media is certainly more positive now than at any point in the last 30 years. In May 1997, the *Scotsman*, which had carried the stories about Dundee's depressing image in the 1960s and 70s, reported 'Dundee has never looked better and is promoting itself with an energy and enthusiasm others could do well to copy'. But is it just the perception of Dundee that is improving or is Dundee really a better place now for ordinary people than it was in 1945? Most would say it is – but the situation is perhaps summed up by quoting the spry old worthy who paused for breath while peching up the Hilltown and asserted with a grin that 'as long as Dundee doesn't start to believe her own hype, she will do just fine.' As she always has done and most likely always will on the long roller-coaster ride of history.

Appendix

Figure 1

Dundee's War Dead 1939–45

The estimated total of 1,899 includes (all services): Privates 411; Sergeants 216; Gunners 99; Able seamen 88; Lance Corporals 73, Flight Sergeants 53; Sappers 41; Leading Aircraftmen 40; Lieutenants 37; Ordinary seamen 36; Drivers 34; Guardsmen 26; Pilot Officers 23; Signalmen 19; Flying Officers 17; Flight Lieutenants 16; Chief Engineering Officers 15; Captains 12; Squadron Leaders 4; Majors 2; Female service personnel 6 and a Wing Commander, Lieutenant Commander, Lieutenant Colonel and Colonel.

Place of death: at sea 435; in Western Europe 304; Far East 114; Italy 145; Middle East 177; Africa 76; unknown locations 65; in Dundee (civilians) 4.

(This is a selection, not a complete listing)

Source: City of Dundee Roll of Honour, with thanks to the research of Mr John T. Foy.

Figure 2

Dundee's Population, selected years from 1939–2001

1939 mid year estimate	178,013
1940	165,000
1951	177,340
1961	182,978
1971*	197,371
1981*	179,674
1991#	156,240
1995#	151,010
1999#	144,430
2001+	142,532

Sources:

1939–1961 from Third Statistical Account, 1979

* Census 1981

G.R.O.S. Mid-year populations

+ G.R.O.S. 1998-based projection

Figure 3

Car Ownership 1981-91

	1981	1991
Households no car	38,151	37,325
One car	23,812	26,602
Two cars	4,681	⎰8,273⎱
Three or more cars	708	

Source: Census 1981, 1991

Figure 4

Unemployment, selected years 1939–2002

	Dundee	Scotland
1939	13.5%	13.5%
1953	2.7	3.0
1956	3.0	2.4
1957	4.5	2.6
1961	3.5	3.5
1964	2.2	3.4
1971 (May)	7.0	9.1
1981 (June)	15.5	13.5
1986 (Aug)	16.5	15.6
1991 (Nov)	10.6	10.3
1996	10.9	8.9
1997	9.7	7.4
1998	9.2	6.6
1999	8.6	6.2
2000	8.2	5.8

Sources: 1939–71 Third Statistical Account of Scotland, 1979, 1981–1991 Dept of Employment figures, 1996–2000, NOMIS. NB: The method of counting varies; 1953–1981 was based on National Insurance, 1996–2000 was based on Claimant Count monthly averages.

Figure 5
Housing Tenure by type, 1991

Owner Occupier	42%
Private Landlord	6.6
Rented Council House	41.8
Scottish Homes	3.9
Rented Housing Assoc	4.9
Tied with job or business	0.8

Source: Census 1991

Figure 6

Dundee Housing by type, 1991

Detached	7.5%
Semi-detached	15.9
Terraced	15.5
Purpose built flat	59.6
Converted accommodation	1.5
Other	0.1

Source: Census 1991

Figure 7

Dundee's Socio-Economic Profile, 1991

I	Professional Occupations	6.3%
II	Managerial & Technical	23.3
III	Skilled, non-manual	14.6
IV	Partly skilled	30.7
V	Unskilled	6.7
	Forces	0.3
	Govt Scheme	1.2
	Other	0.9

Source: Census 1991

Figure 8

Comparison of Employment by Industry Sector, 1997

Industry	Dundee	Aberdeen	Edinburgh	Scotland	UK
Manufacturing	16.8	11.4	9.0	18.0	16.4
Construction	5.3	5.9	3.3	5.6	4.4
Service sector	22.2	21.4	20.4	22.7	22.8
Transport & Communications	4.4	6.2	5.4	5.3	5.9
Banking & Finance	12.0	19.1	25.0	14.8	18.6
Public Administration, Education & Health	34.1	20.1	30.3	27.6	24.4
Other services sectors	4.8	3.7	5.1	4.9	4.7

Source: Annual Employment Survey 1997

Figure 9

Comparison of Average Gross Weekly Full-Time Earnings, 1998

Dundee	male £389.9	female £296.6	average £354.2
Aberdeen	484.2	310.9	423.2
Edinburgh	438.8	333.6	396.1
Glasgow	413.8	308.9	373.1
Scotland	406.0	297.7	364.9
UK	442.4	326.5	400.1

Source: Office for National Statistics, New Earnings Survey 1999

Figure 10

Lord Provosts of Dundee 1940-2002

Dundee Corporation

November 1940	Garnet Wilson (Liberal)
November 1946	Archibald Powrie (Socialist) [d. 12 January 1949]
February 1949	John C. Adamson (Socialist)
May 1949	Richard Fenton (Moderate)
May 1952	William Black (no affiliation)
May 1954	William Hughes (Socialist)
May 1960	Maurice McManus (Labour)
May 1967	Alexander Mackenzie (Labour)
May 1970	William K. Fitzgerald (Progressive)
May 1973	Thomas W. Moore (Labour)

Dundee District Council

May 1974	Charles D.P. Farquhar (Labour)
May 1977	Henry W.C. Vaughan (Progressive)
May 1980	James P. Gowans (Labour)
May 1984	Thomas Mitchell(Labour)
May 1992	Thomas McDonald (Labour) [d. 22 June 1995]
June 1995	Norman McGowan (Labour)

Dundee City Council

April 1996	Mervyn Rolfe (Labour)
May 1999	Helen Wright(Labour)
June 2001	John Letford (Labour)

Source: Local Studies, Dundee Central Library.

Figure 11

Political Representation: MPs, MSPs, MEP

| 1945 | T.F. Cook (Soc) |
| | E.J. Strachey (Soc) |

	Dundee East	Dundee West
1950	T.F. Cook (Soc)	E.J. Strachey (Soc)
1951	T.F. Cook (Soc) died	E.J. Strachey (Soc)
	George Thomson (Soc, by-elec)	
1955	George Thomson (Soc)	E.J. Strachey (Soc)
1959	George Thomson (Soc)	E.J. Strachey (Soc) died
Nov 1963		Peter Doig (Lab, by-elect)
1964	George Thomson (Lab)	Peter Doig (Lab)
1966	George Thomson (Lab)	Peter Doig (Lab)
1970	George Thomson (Lab) ret	Peter Doig (Lab)
1973	George Machin (Lab, by-elec)	Peter Doig (Lab)
Feb 1974	Gordon Wilson (SNP)	Peter Doig (Lab)
Oct 1974	Gordon Wilson (SNP)	Peter Doig (Lab) ret
1979	Gordon Wilson (SNP)	Ernest Ross (Lab)
1983	Gordon Wilson (SNP)	Ernest Ross (Lab)
1987	John McAllion (Lab)	Ernest Ross (Lab)
1992	John McAllion (Lab)	Ernest Ross (Lab)
1997	John McAllion (Lab)	Ernest Ross (Lab)
2001	Ian Luke (Lab)	Ernest Ross (Lab)

Scottish Parliament 'Directly-Elected' MSPs

| 1999 | John McAllion (Lab) | Kate McLean (Lab) |

Scottish Parliament: North-East Scotland 'List' MSPs

1999	Shona Robison (SNP)
	Irene McGugan (SNP)
	Richard Lochhead (SNP)
	Brian Adam (SNP)
	Alex Johnstone (Cons)
	Ben Wallace (Cons)
	David Davidson (Con)

European Parliament, North East Scotland MEP

| 1998 | Ian Hudghton (SNP) |

Source: Local Studies, Dundee Central Library.

Selected
Bibliography

Dorward, **David** *Dundee: Names, People & Places* Mercat Press, 1989.

Hendry, **Jan** *Dundee Greats* John Donald, 1991.

Horan, **Martin** *Kings, Gods and Commoners* Kings' Theatre Trust/Walton Services, 2001.

Horsey, **Miles, and Geoffrey Stell** (eds.) *Dundee On Record: Images of the Past* HMSO, 1992.

Howe, **Stewart** *William Low & Co: A Family Business History* Abertay Historical Society, 2000.

Jeffrey, **Andrew** *This Dangerous Menace* Mainstream, 1991.

Kay, **Billy** (cd.) *The Dundee Book* Mainstream (1990), 1995.

Kelly, **Pat** *Dundee United Who's Who* John Donald, 1998.

Kelly, **Pat** *Rags to Riches, The Official History of Dundee United* Winters, 1992.

McKean, **Charles, and David Walker** *Dundee: An Illustrated Introduction* RIAS (1984), 1993.

Marshall, **Peter** *The Railways of Dundee* Oakwood Press, 1996.

Murray, **Janice, and David Stockdale** *Dundee At Work* Sutton, 1995.

Murray, **Janice, and David Stockdale** *The Miles Tae Dundee* Dundee Art Galleries, 1990.

Ogilvy, **Graham** (ed.) *Dundee: Voyage of Discovery* Mainstream, 1999.

Ogilvy, **Graham** (ed.) *The River Tay and its People* Mainstream, 1993.

Scott, **Andrew Murray** *Discovering Dundee* Mercat Press (1989), 1999.

Watson, **Mike** *The Tannadice Encyclopaedia* Mainstream, 1997.

Whatley, **C.A. and D. Swinfen, A. Smith** *The Life and Times of Dundee* John Donald, 1993.

Wilkie, **Jim** *Across The Great Divide: A History of Professional Football In Dundee* Mainstream, 1984.

Wilkie, **Jim** *Blue Suede Brogans*; *Scenes from a Secret Life of Scottish Rock Music* Mainstream, 1991.

Wilkie, **Jim** *Bonetti's Blues: Dundee FC and its cultural experiment* Mainstream, 2001.

Index